Unraveling the Mysteries of Marketing

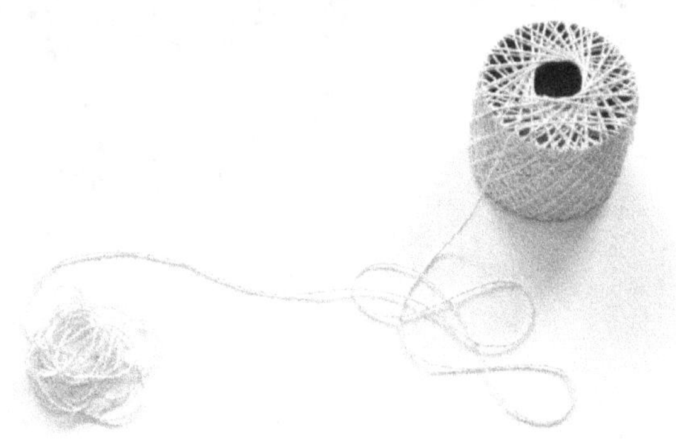

Listening
Cliche
Extraordinary Easy
Storytelling Samples
Optimism Fearlessness
Focus Questions Autopilot
Active Targeting
Blank Perception Networking
Price Promises
Exuberance Brand
Radar

Reader Reviews

Timely and Timeless Wisdom

"Jeff Slater is a magical story-teller and has the unique gift of weaving in pearls of wisdom among the engaging storyline. His insights on marketing are both completely up to date (timely) and likely to stand the test of time (timeless)."

Don P

Informative and useful

"Each of the 21 chapters focuses on a theme encapsulated by a single word; Focus, Targeting, Perception, Fearlessness etc. Following the story and a discussion of its relevance, every chapter concludes with a short summary of the key learning points and at least 1 challenge/suggestion to the reader."

Joe H

A Treasure Trove of Insights and Practical Advice

"Jeff weaves his life's stories into powerful lessons on how to get your brand noticed in a way that sticks and resonates with customers and makes you laugh along the way. He generously shares a lifetime of wisdom about a topic he has forgotten more about than most of us collectively know."

Bob S

Wit and Wisdom, a Perfect Combination

"I am an experienced and educated marketer and entrepreneur and I learned more reading Unraveling the Mysteries of Marketing, than I did getting my MBA!"

Dana C

A little gem

"Slater has created a gem of a book: practical, easy to grasp, and valuable for those trying to get a handle on something (marketing) that for many (such as this reviewer) doesn't come as second nature."

Sephage

A book for the non-marketing expert!
"A fast and interesting read that gives you the quick ins and outs on a subject we THINK we know about."
Milo F

Stories from a storyteller
"Besides building and selling a successful business, Jeff had the opportunity to hang out with Ronald Reagan and Randy `Macho Man' Savage. I want to know what he knows."
Chris D

An excellent read, regardless of your background
"Jeff effortlessly provides the reader with invaluable life and business lessons with every story he tells. Each lesson is infused with humor and practical guidance that is sure to benefit any reader, no matter their background."
Tony P

Valuable lessons & fun to read
"I found the principles Jeff teaches in this book to be really helpful guiding posts for navigating the world of marketing."
Candace H

Great Stories connect you to your customer,
"Through my years of experience in marketing and selling, the message is clear that telling a story and making a human connection to your customer is the key to success. In his book Jeff Slater has provided solid marketing advice while sharing his life journey. It's worth the read."
S. McClendon

TABLE OF CONTENTS

Copyright Information

TITLE: Unraveling the Mysteries of Marketing

Copyright: **Jeffrey Lynn Slater**

Published: September 15, 2013

Publisher: Jeffrey Lynn Slater

Author Photo: Dan Glasgow
www.danglasgow.com

Cover Design: Jeff Lawson
http://www.cowangraphicdesign.com/

PREFACE

Over the last 30 years, my life has revolved around stories about **family, food and marketing**. I love unraveling the threads of these tales to bring personal experiences to life and to teach clear and simple lessons about important moments in my life.

I wondered if I could help the community of marketing novices who are *hungry* to unravel some of the mysteries of marketing by telling a few stories from my marketing career. In this book, I share many special lessons learned with my own *eureka* moment that highlight important ideas about successful marketing.

These lessons didn't occur in a classroom. They happened in the real and at times *surreal*, world through interactions with a wide range of both famous and not-so-famous people. I learned from a **President of the United States named Reagan**, a professional wrestler named **Macho Man Randy Savage** and the exotically strange and wonderful **Frank Zappa**. During my marketing journey, I came to understand how much you can learn about business and marketing by being in the moment.

Looking back, I realize that my marketing adventures were meant to teach, to inspire and eventually be shared with others interested in understanding marketing. **Each story is wrapped with a single key marketing lesson, concept or insight that has helped me learn an important brand building strategies or a practical tactic.** When you combine these stories together, they are like preparing a meal where each ingredient is blended together to create a sweet and delicious experience.

There are plenty of textbooks and how-to-books available where you can also learn some of these principles. **This book is different.**

I am an experienced entrepreneur who has done exactly what you want to do - successfully – use marketing to grow a brand and to create an emotional bond between your product and your customers. Each example in this marketing memoir is filled with personal anecdotes embedded with crisp, clear information that you can use to improve your own communications efforts. **My sincere hope is that this book will *spark* your creativity and assist as you successfully build your brand and grow your business.**

Within each individual story I extracted a key word or phrase as a marketing lesson. In simple and straightforward language, these key words can help guide you in your entrepreneurial venture or small to mid-sized business.

The book will answer marketing questions such as…

Why you must **differentiate** your brand from the category to be noticed and to have the market share your story.

Why **asking questions** is one of most powerful way to market and sell a product or service.

Fearlessness is a critical requirement to help you get to the next level of success.

Optimism plays a surprising role in all marketing activities.

Being on **auto pilot** can be deadlier for a brand than a wrong decision. Never stay on cruise control.

How **storytelling** can build depth and emotional connection to your brand or product.

Why is it vital to your brand's health that you are highly **focused**?

How you can learn an extraordinary lesson about **word of mouth** from something as simple as superb fried chicken.

Those who have studied marketing in business school may not find my approach of great value although I hope they will be amused by some of my life stories. Some might be critical that I have over-simplified marketing. I accept that at face value and this book is not for you.

I am sharing my experiences without the artifice of fancy language and complex words. I have tried to tell my story with a clear voice so the reader can use many of these lessons in growing their own business.

My goal is modest. I only want my marketing memoir to help one person: YOU.

Do you get marketing? Is this subject really clear to you? *Are you often confused or intimidated by marketing speak and marketing mumbo jumbo?* If so, this book can be helpful.

Are you someone who needs a marketing coach, a sounding board or even a spark of inspiration to help them marketing their products or services? If so, then the lessons I share may be of value.

Whether you own a small business owner, work as a Director of Marketing at a small to mid-sized business or work at a non-profit, **Unraveling The Mysteries of Marketing** is **rich with specific actions you can take** to take your marketing to the next level.

My background

During the past 30 years, I have spent half my career as an entrepreneur and half in corporate marketing roles. The wonderful irony is that I never took any business classes with the exception of Economic 101 at The Wharton School, fulfilling my fathers' request. My interests in college and graduate school were in the social sciences, art history and communications. I expected to be a professional photographer like my maternal grandfather George Ginsberg. But as fate would have it, I ended up helping my wife with her growing brownie baking business in Philadelphia in the late 1970's. This business, **Rachel's Brownies**, was almost an afterthought for two college-educated twenty somethings who didn't know what to do with their lives as we stumbled down a chocolate brick road.

Rated the Best Brownies in Philadelphia in 1976 by Philadelphia Magazine, which turned it into an overnight success, Ra El went from baking and selling a few hundred brownies a week for almost two years to our making and marketing over two hundred thousand brownies a day over the next decade. I quit my day job selling advertising for a magazine to put on an apron and wear many entrepreneurial hats as president of the company and head of sales, marketing, and product research. Ra El remained in charge of every aspect of quality control as chairwoman of the board. Our business expanded with customers like Bloomingdales, People Express Airlines, United Airlines, Publix Supermarket and Wawa convenience stores in Philadelphia. As our business exploded, we landed on Inc. Magazine's fastest growing businesses in 1985. We were featured on numerous national TV shows, newspapers, magazines and books. Eventually we sold the company to a much larger food endeavor named GoodMark Foods in North Carolina who owns bakeries, packaged meats and the iconic Slim Jim brand. When we sold our business, the management at GoodMark Foods wanted me to be responsible for the marketing of their bakery brands and to help inject an entrepreneurial spirit into the business.

Truth be told, I had no idea what marketing was at that time.

I never read a marketing book and didn't take any classes in college or graduate school to prepare me for a marketing career. During college and graduate school at The University of Pennsylvania, my interests were in subjects as wide as communications, anthropology and art history.

Regarding business, I did have a keen sense of how important it was to make an extraordinary product, be authentic and to inspire a tribe of loyal followers. Remember this was in the 1970's and 1980's and predated The Internet. Our Rachel's Brownie community wasn't on Facebook but met us face to face as they came to our bakery in Malvern, Pennsylvania in search of an intense chocolate connection. Our brand had a special secret advantage in the remarkable skills that my wife Ra El had in maintaining impeccable standards of quality control and product integrity with uncompromising dedication to perfection, as well as the original recipe and beautiful handwritten label that she created in 1975. An artist and musician at heart, Ra El started the business as a way to make some extra money, and marketing was the last thing on her mind. It turns out that hyper focus on details, quality, integrity, and a personal touch was all she ever needed to start the business. As she said to President Reagan, "it had to be perfect. It had my name on every brownie."

From this ad hoc business education, I started to become intrigued with the art and science of marketing. I read voraciously, talked with as many professionals as possible and learned from any business executive who would talk with me. My late father, Jack Slater a financial executive for Triangle Industries, Merrill Lynch and Smith Barney, did attend The Wharton School at The University of Pennsylvania in 1948. He guided me on my path with the patience of a saint and the love of a proud father. My grandfather George Ginsberg also nurtured whatever creative talents I possessed as he regaled me with tales of marketing his commercial photo business, Quaker Photo in Philadelphia in the 1930's. While my beloved Aunt Annette would cheer us on, even my mother helped as she and her best friend Norma delivered brownies in New Jersey to such landmark shops as Millburn Deli and King's Supermarkets.

I was also fortunate that I could confer with a top marketing executive, Robert Subin at Campbell's soup. Bob developed the Prego brand and was an informal advisor that gave me a peak into the corporate world of marketing. His advice was mmm mmm good.

After selling our business, my career and responsibilities expanded at GoodMark as over time I become an Executive Vice President at one of the largest snack food companies in the country. I went from having $30 to spend on marketing and sales to $30,000,000. With this fund, I was responsible for national television commercials, sponsorship with Professional Wrestling (Macho Man Randy Savage), NASCAR (Bobbie and Terry Labonte) and The X Games Extreme Sports (Dave Mirra), celebrity endorsements, sponsorship of country music festival promotions (George Strait, Tim McGraw, and The Dixie Chicks) and on and on. It was quite a ride.

Fortunately I was acutely aware of how special each moment was and I truly savored these extraordinary experiences. Best of all, I was surrounded by so many colleagues and agencies who were so much smarter than me that I had a chance to learn something new every single day. I recognize my good fortune to have been surrounded by teachers who had a passion for marketing equal to my own.

Today I hold the title of Global Director of Marketing for Nomacorc. We sell wine closures and our corcs (not corks) close over 2.5 billion bottles of wine throughout the world. In this position, I have had the great opportunity to expand my marketing horizons working internationally and continue to learn from some extraordinarily smart colleagues and agency partners.

It is my sincere hope to that the ideas and information in this book will help you achieve your marketing goals. If you become aware of the lessons right in front of you every day, then I have succeeded. I hope this collection of personal stories helps to unravel some of the mysteries of marketing. *Won't you come along for the journey?*

Who Should Read This Book?

If you are an experienced marketer with an MBA from an expensive business school, this book is NOT for you. There are plenty of wonderful marketing books that you should read that will build upon your base of knowledge. Check out my blog MomentSlater for a listing of fabulous marketing books that I have reviewed for someone who has worked in marketing and is looking to expand their knowledge and open up to some counter intuitive thinking. I write about authors like Youngme Moon, Simon Sinek, Jay Baer, Tim Brown, Douglas Van Praet and many other experts.

If marketing is a bit of a mystery to you, this book is for you. Whether you are a small business owner or are new and inexperienced in marketing, this may be the right book for you to read. It is filled with easy to understand ideas about marketing that are told through the personal stories of an entrepreneur who successfully grew a small business and then continued working in several large and mid-sized companies managing marketing.

Do you struggle with these questions?

How can marketing profitably grow my business?

Should I add a new line of product to my business?

Why don't I have more customers?

How important is it to be focused on one unique benefit for customers?

Is it a good idea to partner with other businesses?

Should I use traditional advertising to get customers or is there a better way to be found?

How come I don't get more potential customers to my website?

Can I learn how to stand out from my competitors?

Am I pricing my offerings properly?

How can I understand my customer's needs better?

Think of this book like a marketing coach for someone who knows they need to market their business but doesn't understand the fundamentals and thinks marketing means advertising. (Hint: It doesn't)

Read this book if you want to learn some valuable lessons from a trusted advisor who has been in your shoes without a traditional marketing education. I promise you will learn marketing tools that can help you grow your business. Let me be your guide, your coach and your mentor to unravel the mysteries of marketing.

ABOUT THE AUTHOR

I have more than 30 years of business experience as both an entrepreneur as well as working in the corporate world. Often counter-intuitive, I strive to find a new way to view marketing issues. Sharing what I have learned is a privilege and an honor.

Background
With my wife, we built a nationally recognized wholesale bakery business called **Rachel's Brownies**. National publicity included articles in *The New York Times, USA Today* and *Philadelphia Magazine.* We also appeared on **CNN, The Phil Donahue Show, Charlie Rose** and many others national and syndicated talk shows. We even made **INC Magazine's** list of fastest growing business in 1985. Who knew you could make a living selling brownies?

The company was successfully sold in 1989 to GoodMark Foods in Raleigh, North Carolina where I initially managed all of their bakery businesses. Over time, I rose to the position of Executive Vice President of Marketing for their $400 million snack food company with $100 million brands that included Slim Jims and David's Sunflower Seeds. I had the great joy of creating commercials with the late Macho Man Randy Savage and even got to teach him how to use email! *Oh yeah!*

I was responsible for GoodMark's $20 million marketing, advertising and promotion budgets including the highly successful, "Snap into a Slim Jim" campaign from the late 1990's. (Credit for the creative work goes to Hal Rosen and The Steve's from our advertising agency). The extraordinary team I managed worked on sponsorships and event marketing like The X Games, national music tours with George Strait, Tim McGraw and The Dixie Chicks and even created a unique event for teens called Rebelliache. It was a never ending learning experience for me and I got to work with some of the most skilled professional marketing agencies and colleagues. GoodMark was sold to ConAgra in 2003. Every moment was a chance to learn from the best in the business and I look back fondly at those memories.

Today I am employed as the Global Director of Marketing for Nomacorc in Zebulon, North Carolina. Nomacorc is the leading brand of still wine closures with 2.5 billion corks sold in 2012. Once again I get to work with incredibly smart and talented colleagues from around the world. In case you are wondering, I am a big fan of Italian red wines especially when they have our closure on them.

Personal Life

I earned a BA with Honors from The University of Pennsylvania in Communications, an MA from The Annenberg School of Communications and took advanced communications classes at Harvard University. During my career, I have been honored to be a guest lecturer at The University of Pennsylvania, N.C. State and University of Dijon Business School in Burgundy, France along with countless other appearances at symposiums, conferences and marketing panel discussions.

I am an avid cook with a passion for fresh ingredients and rich flavors. Julia Child is in my pantheon of teachers. I also spent many years as a commercial photographer and still love to take pictures. I write about early entrepreneurs like my grandfather George Ginsberg who would have invented the Original Facebook 50 years ago had the technology existed. Jazz is the soundtrack for my life and Ella Fitzgerald is another one of my personal guides through the universe.

DEDICATION

This book is dedicated to several people who have taught me the lessons of patience, creativity and love.

My grandparents: George and Fannie Ginsberg and Joseph and Gertrude Slater. A strand of each one is embedded in my DNA. Poppa George's super powers of creativity, Grandma Fannie's love of the simple things, Poppa Joey's generosity and Grandma Gertie's ability to use food as a magnet to pull a family together.

My Parents: My late father Jack Slater who is so present with me each and every day that I can feel his love and the gentle power of his kindness supporting every moment in my life. Although he left the material world, he remains my guiding light.

My 86 year old Mom Bea Slater who reminds me every day that you are never too old to learn something new or to eat ice cream. In the past three years she has mastered email, Facebook and attended a Bruce Springsteen concert with my brother Mitch. And, she is now learning to use the iPhone to text and FaceTime with family. During the early years of my marketing career, she and her best friend Norma Schaffer were distributors in New Jersey of our brownies. My mother inspires to be happy in each moment of every day. If I am ever not feeling well or sad, her sage advice was to take a shower and you will always feel better.

My siblings Diane (and her husband Jerry) and Mitch (and his wife Leslie) have always cheered me on through each step on the ladder of life. I am so fortunate to learn from their love and generosity. I am truly blessed with brothers and sisters who have always been available to me with open hearts and loving kindness. We are family.

To my nieces and nephews: Thank you to my talented and resourceful nieces and nephews who have always reflected back to me so much love, respect and an appreciation of family.

To my late Aunt Annette: Few people get to touch your life so much that they get extra credit for shaping who you are. My beloved late Aunt Annette was the person who would sit with me on a Saturday afternoon and play scrabble or teach me how to water color. She would explain the high art of Opera and the low-brow fun of Laurel and Hardy. Most of all she put a spatula in my hand and encouraged me to cook. She gave me my first introduction to Julia Child and was a powerful teacher of what it means to be present with another person. In the pantheons of cheerleading, she was always singing my praise even if it wasn't truly deserved. She would be so proud that I am writing a book. I aspire to craft words and language with the exquisite skills you possessed. I was so fortunate to be caught by Annette.

To my professional colleagues who taught me about marketing, life and the encouragement to always move forward, I am indebted. There are so many to name but two require special mentions: George and Britt, thank you for your patience and grace and the gift of your wisdom and friendship.

To my childhood best friend: Jamie, you make me laugh and remind me that the #32, Frank Zappa and salami cooked in a dustpan will always have special meaning.

To my daughters, Sarah and Fanny, you have given me a gift every moment of your lives. Knowing that you are smart, creative and compassionate women of limitless talents makes me happy beyond words. Thank you for choosing me as your father in this lifetime and for nourishing my soul. You both inspire me to keep learning and to never stop being silly.

Our daughters are both remarkable women too. Our older daughter **Sarah** lives on Oahu near Honolulu and teaches AP Psychology, personal development and leadership skills, and teen counseling at The Punahou School. She is also a certified yoga instructor and teaches young girls about stretching toward their dreams with self-love and compassion. You can learn about her program here at her Facebook page Summer Yoga for Teen Girls.

Our younger daughter **Fanny** is an improv performer turned entrepreneur and chef and has created a business called Fanfare Catering in Wilmington, North Carolina. She offers cooking classes, catering for corporate lunches and other business and personal events, personal chef services, and writes a monthly article about food for Focus on the Coast Magazine. Check out her blog at Fanfare Foodie.

To my wife Ra El is an accomplished artist, writer, musician, spiritual teacher and healer who is the most courageous person I have ever known. Her ability to serve as an intuitive guide and channel for divine wisdom vibrates on frequencies that few have experienced. Those who know her well recognize the limitless depth of her compassion and ever present lovingkindness that emanates from her heart and soul. She is truly a messenger of light, currently at work on her first book about awakening the divine heart of humanity. I witness life-affirming lessons every day by being near her as we celebrate our love in life's quiet moments. We have been married since 1977 and are blessed with our two exceptional daughters Sarah and Fanny.

FOCUS

CHAPTER ONE: FOCUS

THE POWER OF FOCUS IN MARKETING

I am good at staying focused on priorities. It isn't that I am not open to new information or ideas, but I am aware that I don't ever have the time or resources to do everything.

I speak from experience.

Thirty years ago when my wife and I had our wholesale bakery business, we made one product: brownies. For fourteen years, we didn't diversify into wholesaling muffins, breads or cookies. Just brownies. For a short period we dabbled and did stray into other items but quickly realized we should stick to our chocolate strength and be #1 in something instead of #8 in everything. We knew that the focus on one product made us the expert. And, by virtue of our hyper focus, we developed a recipe for success. Our brand stood for one thing- *kick ass brownies.*

During my entrepreneurial days, I usually had about $30 to spend on marketing and not enough help to get things done. In some of my past consumer packaged goods positions, I got to work with $30,000,000 budgets and a team of 12 marketing professionals. Even with all that support, I still didn't have enough people, money or time to do all that was asked.

Focus is the key to my success. I quickly started to learn that the problem wasn't too few resources, it was too many needs. Whether it is managing brands or managing my time and resources, the best lesson I ever learned was the extraordinary importance of the F word. FOCUS.

What was required in my marketing roles was to put as much of our team's energy against the few most important efforts that could affect a change in the market. And I was always on the forefront of resisting dumb ideas like line extensions, brand creep and other activities that caused us to weaken and dilute our brand. Brand creep is the idea that your name can be spread like mayonnaise on ever product and category. In consumer marketing, this is a real problem.

Marketing is Math

It is the nature of marketing and brand building, to divide not to multiply to get stronger. The best book on this subject is by Al Ries from the 1990's- it is simply called FOCUS and worth reading. I have read it about eleven times.

In this book, Ries discusses how powerful brands that stand for something lose their meaning when they get spread over too many categories. Xerox brand was powerful representing copiers. Then they spread that name on computers and weakened what they stood for in the mind of the consumer.

Airlines notoriously tried to be all things to all people and stood for nothing whereas the focused airline, Southwest stood for only one thing and followed through on their message of value. No assigned seating, no first class, no food, simple pricing structure and they had a clear plan just to concentrate their efforts on business travel not leisure destinations. They used the same planes on all routes which cut back on stocking spare parts and training and allowed them to better manage complexity and cost. And Southwest is one of a few profitable businesses due in large part to a clear and well-defined brand.

When you think coffee store you think Starbucks, yet how many places served coffee pre-1975? But no one specialized in it and became the expert. Being an expert requires the power of saying no to lots of distractions so that your brand can mean something important. Consumers drive past plenty of places that sell inexpensive coffee, like 7-11, Dunkin Donuts and McDonalds, to get to a Starbucks.

Volvo owned the word safety when it came to cars. It stood for something. And then they got this stupid idea they should make sports cars and compete with BMW and Audi. How can a car be both a family car that protects your kids and a high performance machine to drive on the autobahn?

Answer: It can't be both things at the same time.

Now if Volvo thinks that it needs a performance car in this category, than go create a product and brand that stands for that in the mind of consumers instead of diluting the Volvo brand. Toyota and Lexus are the best example of doing this correctly where each brand represents a different offering in the good/better and best approach to branding.

Staying Focused: Marketers have to prioritize and bring focus to our work. Being a trained photographer, the word focus has meaning that parallels my business world experience. A lens that slowly racks into focus helps you clearly see your target and to capture it. The blurry images that pass by are not mission critical and need to be ignored. You can't just sit back and watch what develops. *Snap into it.*

Brands can't have one foot in two camps at the same time.

If your industry has three key players all with unique benefits to their customers, you will find one of the three who suddenly decides that instead of focusing deeper, they give up and 'sleep with the enemy'. They dip a toe in the water of their competitor's space and start hurting their brands meaning. Stay focused on your strengths and find ways to innovate within their subcategory so that you can reinforce your expertise and don't water it down.

Be an expert and not a generalist.

Think of a medical situation. If you have to get open heart surgery, I bet you aren't going to ask your general practitioner to operate on you. You want someone who has done this procedure over and over again and who is clearly an expert. It is the same thing with a product or service. Don't you want to buy shoes from someone whose brand's represents expertise in the arts and craft of shoe making?

Do you get a haircut from your gardener?

Do you ask your plumber to help you wire your light switch?

Do you ask your insurance agent to help you with a legal matter?

And depending on the nature of the legal matter, there are all types of experts with sub niches to serve you best. You must stand for something and be seen as having deep expertise even if it is in a narrow niche. The expert always wins and your brand must be #1 in something.

TESTING 1, 2, 3

If your business is highly focused in a clearly defined niche, how can you manage all of the daily distractions and get the important stuff done? I like to use a simple test to make sure that I am focused on the right things for my business.

First, **am I spending at least 85% of my time and money on the top three priorities?** These priorities could be outreach to new customers, networking to build partnerships or blogging to drive traffic to my site. Less than 85% means I probably will be failing on at least one of them because it is difficult to concentrate on more than three big things at one time.

Steven Covey refers to this as concentrating on moving the 3 big rocks in front of you- not the 25 little pebbles. He also reminds you that if you were landing a plane, you would probably want to focus on the three most important things going on- not all the other distractions.

Second, **do I have 15% of my time and money to experiment?** Every budget or time management class will teach you that you need a little room to play. Maybe you want to experiment with a new tactic or test the waters with a different market to reach. 15% of your marketing funds or other resources give you a chance to try a few small experiments. More than that and it becomes a distraction. Less, and you feel boxed in a little too much. 15% gives me wiggle room.

Third, and perhaps most importantly, **am I saying no often enough to distraction, dilution and off-strategy requests?** You have to say no to the onslaught of focus-killing ideas that come your way. Why don't we do more here, why can't we spend more there? Let's spread ourselves a little thinner until we don't have enough to do anything effectively?

No is the most powerful weapon in a marketers arsenal because it reinforces what you stand for and the work you need to accomplish for success. If your brand has secondary meaning in the marketplace, saying no allows you to stay focused. When you say yes often, you are probably going astray, getting distracted and setting yourself up for failure.

As I plan my work each day, I look at my list of tasks and spend as much time as I can trying to move the needle of my top three projects. And in a professional way, I say no often when my focus is diverted.

Remember as a kid taking a magnifying glass outside and by harnessing the sun, you could burn a hole in a leaf? Marketing is no different. **Focus is the most powerful brand building light you can shine.**

FOCUS

This may be the most important marketing lesson I can share. Your business needs focus on a clearly defined market. You have to work with great concentration on that objective too.

If you are constantly chasing the bright shiny objects that distract, you can't possibly move forward and execute your priorities. Put the time and effort into a plan with a prioritized list of activities. Sort them so that you know the three most important efforts and budget most of your time to get them done right.

Focus means saying no often. It means asking your boss or colleagues... "How does this new activity fit with our strategy and top priorities"? Everything can't be first. Everything can't be urgent and critical.

Focus means you are constantly searching for the greatest leverage point where your activity has the more significant result to help you achieve your goal. It means having a "not to do list", ignoring daily interruptions and knowing what you must get done to move forward.

Five little letters with a powerful message. Always remember this F word.

TARGETING

CHAPTER TWO: TARGETING

WHAT IS TARGET MARKETING?

Most businesses don't spend enough time thinking about their target market. Often, when I ask people who they are trying to reach with their marketing they describe everyone in broad terms without any clarity or real specificity. They may say woman aged 30-59 who buy hats or men 18-34 who download sports apps or households with income above $50K.

This is way too broad, general and will get you nowhere.

Your target cannot be everyone with a heartbeat. But perhaps you aren't even clear what target marketing is all about.

What exactly is target marketing and why does it matter to my business?

I like to personalize my target as specifically as I can. In fact, I prefer to start with a name and to put as much detail into the profile as possible. One way to do this is to think about an actual customer and to try and describe their world in vivid detail.

In many ways, identifying your target is a lot like Googling information. The more specific you are in your search the better chance you will have to find what you are seeking. Do you Google the word *restaurants*? Or do you Google the word *Authentic Indian restaurant near Raleigh NC 27614?*

Some examples may help.

Recently I have been working on this exercise for my marketing blog called **MomentSlater** trying to identify who is my target audience. Who exactly am I writing this for? How do I describe the specific target audience I am searching to reach with my ideas, comments and observations on marketing? I know that my audience is made up of a few segments of readers so it isn't just one group.

Since I am not selling anything but offering free advice and sharing experiences, it is still relevant to reach as many people as possible who fit my own target. I know that I am writing for relatively inexperienced marketing folks who may own their own small to mid-sized business ($5-$50 million in sales) or people who manage marketing for non-profit organizations. My blog's tagline, like the title of this book, is to unravel the mysteries of marketing. It isn't written for those with an MBA in marketing but instead for someone unsure and unclear about marketing.

Below are three sample targets I am trying to reach. You may end up with several profiles of customers (targets) who have slightly different needs all within a targeted range.

Meet Ken in Financial Services

Ken is in my target audience for my MomentSlater blog. He is a small business owner who offers financial services to clients in need of accounting help, advice on managing inventory or how to plan cash flow. His background is working for 15 years in corporate jobs in accounting and finance but about 3 years ago went off on his own to start his own business.

He is not confident or very knowledgeable about marketing but assumes it has to do with traditional print, radio or TV advertising – which sounds expensive to him. He hasn't thought much about marketing his business since so far he has a few clients keeping him busy. But he isn't growing and doesn't know where to start to build his client base. He networks a little but mostly with people from his past companies.

He reads business publications in print like Inc. Magazine and some accounting journals online that offer some tips on marketing. He realizes that what he needs is a sounding board to guide him through the basics and to lead him in the right direction. He wants to share some of his knowledge for free but is afraid that it will limit his income potential.

Ultimately, what Ken needs is a marketing coach.

Meet Kelly in Graphic Design

Kelly is also in my target audience for the blog. She runs a graphic design firm specializing in creating logos, brand identity and brochures. Most of her work is with clients who she has met through networking and word of mouth recommendations.

Like the cobbler's kid who has no shoes, she isn't really clear how to market herself and her business to others. She thinks that she has some of the basics right but is often too busy working in the business to actually manage the growth of her business. She has tried a few things to get the word out but hasn't found a clear path to success.

Kelly needs someone to give her ideas that she can try to help her expand her base of well-paying clients who value her services and understand what makes her work special. She needs help identifying how to grow her business carefully so she can keep the appropriate focus on her work.

Meet Alex who works at a software start up

Alex is Director of Marketing for a small software startup. He is also in my target audience. He is an employee and is charged with growing awareness, lead generation and promoting the company's brand. He has a little experience in marketing and is really a techie.

He has had some modest success growing the user base but has reached a plateau and needs to take the business to a new level. His past jobs with very large companies didn't prepare him for marketing work so he needs to find low-cost solutions and some new inspiring ideas.

He has strong online knowledge of social media and is very tech savvy but isn't sure where and on what to focus his time and energy to market the company's software. Alex reads a lot of advice columns on marketing but feels like he needs someone in his face, like a personal trainer, regularly to guide his efforts particularly someone who has experience growing a small business.

Alex's greatest need is marketing inspiration that can help spark his own creative juices.

Sounding Board, Coach and Inspirator

From the descriptions of these three people, I have extracted a need for (a) a marketing sounding board, (b) a marketing coach and (c) an inspirator of ideas. This information is helpful to me as it reminds me what my blogs should be about and encourages me to participate in online forums where these topics are being discussed. (LinkedIn Groups for Small Business for example). I can reach more people like Ken, Kelly and Alex by being a sounding board, a coach and an idea inspirator to people like these three targets.

Name your target

Personalize your target. Make them a living and breathing human being. You might even go so far as to use a stand-in picture of that imaginary person and keep it hanging up in your office to remind you who you are focused on reaching. It is so much more helpful to think of your target audience by name since you can start to learn more about their habits, their hobbies and who they are beyond their job.

Your marketing efforts will improve as you personalize who you are trying to reach. Some of this information about your target can come from looking at who your current client base is and who would be similar to them. If you are in a business-to-business marketplace, think about their level of knowledge and sophistication about your area of expertise. How should you speak to them? Are they experts in accounting, graphic design or software? Maybe by thinking about the Ken, Kelly and Alex's in your world, you will realize that you haven't really been providing the right kind of message to your target.

Can you identify a real benefit that you are uniquely qualified to give to them?

If you work in a business to consumer market, the same approach works. Engage with several clients to get to know as much as you can about them. What are their likes and dislikes? What TV or movies do they see, where do they go to eat, where do they shop, what is their favorite book they read last year, how do they get news and information (print, web, TV) and on and on.

What job does your product or service do for them?

For example, you may say sell spa services, but your clients might describe what you do is provide them with mini-vacations. You may offer financial services but what they really want is someone to hold their hand and provide them with comfort. You may sell pesticides to help them get a weed-free lawn but what they really want is the ability to roll around in the grass with their children.

Listen carefully for clues about how you are valued to help you understand how to find more clients who have similar needs. The more you can fill in the blanks, the clearer it will be how you can reach people who share common needs. In understanding your target's needs, think beyond the tangible

thing you sell them (accounting services, logos or apps) and think in terms of the emotional benefit you provide.
Your target audience is made up of individuals. Get to know them just like I am getting to know Ken, Kelly and Alex. As in my own example, don't just provide your target with features; **provide them with benefits that really motivate them to act**.

TARGETING

You cannot sell your product or service to everyone. It is important that you narrowly identify the type of individual who you are trying to reach so that your messaging and how you deliver it fits that individual's need. Targeting requires fine tooth comb not a broad brush if you want to reach the right person.

When you are determining more about your target, think of it as solving a pain point for customers or clients. What precise benefit are you offering someone in your unique way? What is the problem you are solving? This will help you recognize who you want to reach.

Sometimes it is quite counterintuitive. If you are in a business to business selling world, you may need to convince the head of finance that you have the right marketing tools since he may be skeptical of marketing as expensive. And since what you sell is a revolutionary low cost approach, he might be the real target to reach – not the person who runs marketing.

If you sell vitamins for men, it may be that the target's

wife, significant other or his mom may be the target for your message since they may have more influence over what is purchased and brought into the household.

Understand where the target lives (geography), how old they may be (tight and narrow range is best), what type of work they do (job/title), education level, income level and expand your knowledge of their emotional and psychological need for what you have to offer.

If you offer cooking classes in people's homes, your target maybe woman ages 25-34 who want to learn to eat healthier, lives within 20 miles of a specific zip code, work in a professional job and earn $40,000/year. They may also want to learn to cook for emotional reasons so that they can have more control over their life, how they look and how they feel about themselves. A target isn't made of cardboard but flesh, blood and emotions.

Figure out your target but understanding one individual's need not a broad range of people. You'll have more luck if you have a deeper understanding of who they are, what they want and how to reach them.

OPTIMISM

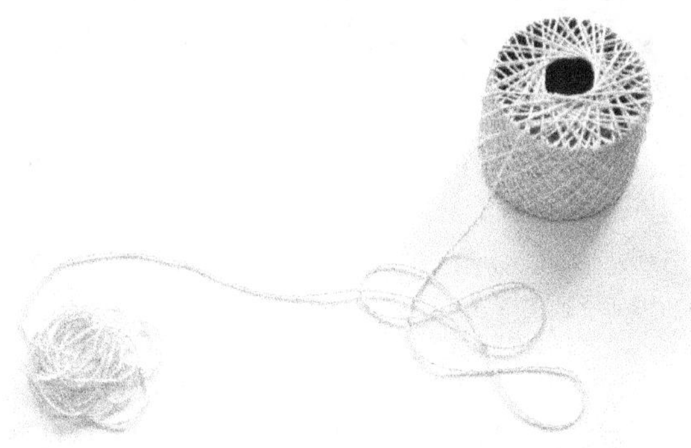

CHAPTER THREE: OPTIMISM

MY LUNCH WITH PRESIDENT RONALD REAGAN

Ever have a really memorable lunch?

I'm not talking about a mouth-watering meal with expensive food, vintage wine or elegant ambiance. Did lunch ever include sharing a meal with someone who works in an oval office?

My wife Ra El and I were living in Pennsylvania and owned a wholesale bakery business that she founded in 1975. The business, Rachel's Brownies was not a planned venture to build the next Sara Lee. She started selling brownies to specialty stores in Philadelphia to help make a few dollars after graduating from Cornell University with a degree in French Literature. I joined after graduating from The University of Pennsylvania in 1976. From the Rocking Horse Ice Cream Parlor to The Fruit Lady's Shop, our brownies were delivered in little wicker baskets with red and white gingham napkins to help create a homemade image. Through a stroke of luck and pure serendipity, Philadelphia Magazine named Rachel's Brownies the best brownies in Philadelphia in 1975. The phone started to ring and the brownies weren't the only thing rising!

Let me mix in a few more bits of information as the story gets richer.

As the business grew we built up quite a following along the Eastern US corridor selling brownies from airlines (United and People Express) to convenience stores (Wawa, 7-11 and AM/PM) to the neighborhood gourmet shop to grocery stores (Kings and Publix). We didn't have Facebook or Blogs to brag about our brownies or to market to a loyal

antithesis of my own. This was someone who I thought wasn't smart enough to be President and I just didn't want to like him.

But *there he goes again*....being the charming remarkable man that people always talk about when they discuss a first-hand experience of meeting him.

He told us stories about his time in Hollywood and some of his experiences during the 1950's making movies in London. He discussed his friendship with people like Henry and Shirlee Fonda, Jimmy and Gloria Stewart and plenty of other A list stars. He made us laugh and he was so authentic and relaxed that it really put us at ease.

We were sitting with the most powerful influential man in the world. Somewhere within a few feet of us was the "football" with the nuclear codes that could launch war. Yet here he was opening up a boxed lunch talking about the movies while examining the contents of his mid-day meal.

Both Ra El and I were dismayed that the gift boxes of brownies we provided to Ron Fuller didn't make it in the boxed lunches. Even a special box for the President that we had the Secret Service put under X-Ray and special scrutiny was nowhere to be seen. Oh well, we figured, let's focus on the positive.

During the meal there were heated conversations about the President's tax plan and several funny stories. About three quarters of the way through the meal a staff member came over to our table and said, Mr. President would you like a brownie?" The President turned and said, "I love brownies - what a treat!"

Our brownies were not the easiest thing to open. In trying to explain to President Reagan the trick of how to get the film off the package, Ra El leaned over and said, Mr. President can

I help unwrap the brownie? Ra El showed him the secret piece of film to pull upon and suddenly the brownie was free

I realized I had an unbelievable opportunity. What if I could get the President to hold up the brownie while I took his picture? What a coup! I remembered that he used to do commercials for all kinds of products
like Chesterfield cigarettes and Van Heusen shirts. Can you image the PR benefit I could get from that photo?

I said Mr President, would you mind if I took your photograph holding our brownie?
He looked at me and without a moment of hesitation said, I'd be happy to have you take a picture. You know, he said, I used to do this for a living.

So I took out my Nikon SLR and started to click away. I knew I should bracket for the light just in case so I got off at least 8 or 9 pictures within a few seconds. But those seconds seemed to last for an hour. *Talk about special moments*...I am taking a photograph of the leader of the free world holding a brownie my wife and I sell in our bakery! The President held the pose like the consummate actor he was and I just clicked and clicked and clicked away.

After this informal photo shoot, the President unwrapped the brownie and took a bite. I remember a glint in his eyes as the rich chocolate trickled down. He savored the brownie and appeared to really enjoy it. He shared how often he eats things that are so fancy and elaborate and that a wonderful brownie is truly a gift.

As the luncheon was breaking up, one of the perfectly hand wrapped boxes of brownies was brought over to Ra El so we could have a photograph taken with the President as we presented the box of brownies. At this moment as we stood up, Ra El said to the President that it was really a thrill and that I look forward to telling this little baby (as she patted her abdomen), that she or he had lunch with the President. The President turned and said, "I didn't know you were pregnant but lots of luck to all of you."

As the President left, Governor Thornburgh came by and said, "I think you have a new devotee for your brownies." Like the President, Governor Thornburgh was a very authentic and warm person.

This exciting day was filled with plenty of interviews on local TV, syndicated radio and newspapers like The Philadelphia Inquirer. We must have done a dozen interviews including a call from a reporter from The New York Times. It was quite a day and we were exhausted.

About two days later, we got a call from CNN asking us to comment on The President's gaffe. I told the reporter that I didn't know what he was talking about. He told me that President Reagan was giving a speech that morning and told the crowd that he met a young couple in Pennsylvania this week and that "Nancy's Brownies were the best he had ever eaten." Obviously, the President made a mistake but that little error kept the news alive about Rachel's Brownies for several more days.

On February 6, 2011, it would have been President Reagan's one hundredth birthday. It is 25 years since that extraordinary lunch took place in an unfinished Meridian Bank building in the suburbs of Philadelphia. Funny how a little chocolate dessert can bridge a gap between a Democrat and a Republican.

Happy 100th birthday President Reagan.

OPTIMISIM

From the French and the Latin "to see the good".

Marketing is centered in optimism. What I witnessed in President Reagan was such a positive and upbeat charisma that it set the tone for both the crowd of thousands and the few dozen people seated at the lunch with him. His optimism was infectious and made others feel like they wanted to hear him and listen to his message. Even I who never voted for a Republican, felt like I should listen to what he had to say because of how he ignited the space with his positive outlook. His optimism felt authentic which only made me more interested in his message.

Reagan famously told a pony joke that illustrated his optimism. "There is so much manure around there must be pony in here somewhere". This is the full pony story...

An excerpt from "How Ronald Reagan Changed My Life" by Peter Robinson

The joke concerns twin boys of five or six. Worried that the boys had developed extreme personalities -- one was a total pessimist, the other a total optimist -- their parents took them to a psychiatrist.

First the psychiatrist treated the pessimist. Trying to brighten his outlook, the psychiatrist took him to a room piled to the ceiling with brand-new toys. But instead of yelping with delight, the little boy burst into tears. "What's the matter?" the psychiatrist asked, baffled. "Don't you want to play with any of the toys?" "Yes," the little boy bawled, "but if I did I'd only break them."

Next the psychiatrist treated the optimist. Trying to dampen his outlook, the psychiatrist took him to a room piled to the ceiling with horse manure. But instead of wrinkling his nose in disgust, the optimist emitted just the yelp of delight the psychiatrist had been hoping to hear from his brother, the pessimist. Then he clambered to the top of the pile, dropped to his knees, and began gleefully digging out scoop after scoop with his bare hands. "What do you think you're doing?" the psychiatrist asked, just as baffled by the optimist as he had been by the pessimist. "With all this manure," the little boy replied, beaming, "there must be a pony in here somewhere!"

"Reagan told the joke so often," Meese said, chuckling, "that it got to be kind of a joke with the rest of us. Whenever something would go wrong, somebody on the staff would be sure to say, "There must be a pony in here somewhere.'"

I carried the lesson from that day with me throughout my career and have found it to be a life affirming inspiration. Reagan was not someone I agreed with but I heard what he had to say. Through his uplifting attitude, I realized that I could be far more effective if I always brought a glass half-full to every marketing moment. Marketers who believe in themselves can infuse a belief in the impossible and can get an audience to listen.

As you market your small business to your customers, an

optimistic and upbeat attitude can be highly influential in being successful. People want to be led and taken on a journey and will follow inspirational individuals. We all can't have Reagan skills, but can you find it in yourself to be affirming, happy and positive in your engagement with your customers?

It may not get you a seat at the table with the President, but it can help you win the votes of new customers.

FEARLESSNESS

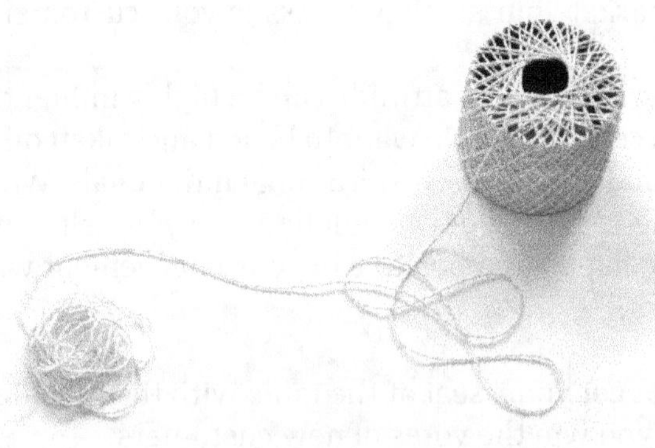

CHAPTER FOUR: FEARLESSNESS

EATING SUSHI WITH BEN AND JERRY

The first time I ever ate raw fish was with Ben Cohen and Jerry Greenfield (AKA Ben and Jerry). Here is the *scoop.*

The year was 1980 and my wife and I were going to the New York Gourmet Specialty Food Show in Manhattan. We didn't have a trade show booth but we thought it would be a good idea to determine if we should exhibit at this type of event so our plan was to walk the show, observe the activity and figure out if we wanted to spend the money to promote our business next year.

The prior month, which I believe was May of 1980, I did something that at the time seem perfectly natural. *I was fearless out of sheer ignorance.* I didn't realize that you couldn't pick up the phone and call someone with semi-celebrity status and actually speak to them.

Out from the cold

I had an idea that maybe we could get Ben and Jerry to use Rachel's Brownies in one of their spectacular ice cream creations. I had *frozen delusions of grandeur* that maybe they would make a Rachel's Brownies ice cream and the publicity from it would help build our brand. *At age 26, I didn't know enough about business to realize what an asset it was to be naive.*

So I picked up the phone and I placed a call to Ben Cohen in Vermont. I told the person who answered the phone that my name was Jeff Slater, I was President of Rachel's Brownies and I wanted to talk to Ben about a wild idea. The receptionist put me through and on the other end of the phone was Ben Cohen. He sounded like an ordinary Joe without any airs about him; none at all.

When I introduced myself and explained about our humble little brownie business in Pennsylvania he said, you guys make Rachel's Brownies. I love Rachel's Brownies; I eat Rachel's Brownies on People Express Airlines all the time. We ought to do an ice cream together!

I froze in my tracks.

You know that feeling you get when you eat ice cream too quickly... a brain freeze? You can picture my amazement that he knew our humble little brownie and actually wanted to connect and he thought the idea was *cool.*

Ben said that he and Jerry were going to be in New York for the Specialty Show and we should get lunch together and talk about this idea. He said he'd call me a day before to figure out a place to meet.

We were hanging out in Springfield, New Jersey at my folks' house the day before the trade show when the phone rings (before cell phone) and it's Ben saying that he knows a neat little restaurant near The New York Public Library. He gave me the name (which I don't remember) and said, *you guys eat sushi right*?

Of course I wanted to be as *hip* as Ben and Jerry so I said, "of course we do."

I'll have the raw fish

Now Ra El and I love to great food and had already eaten things like escargot in Paris so we weren't food rookies but sushi was new to us. In 1980, I am certain we never thought about eating raw fish for lunch but we figured, why not? Worse case we would pick at the pike and taste the tuna...so I confirmed our meeting.

We were to meet on the steps of the New York Public Library and the restaurant was around the corner. I remember thinking since we hadn't met how would I know them? So, I went into my Mom's freezer, took out a pint of coffee Ben and Jerry's, ate the ice cream and cut out the photo on the package - just in case.

I am surprised that I can't find any artifact to share, like a menu or picture from this event. I'm not clever enough to make up a story like this so you'll need to take my word for it that this truly happened.

We met on the steps of the library. I immediately recognized Ben with his trademark hat. He was very garrulous and fun to talk with while Jerry seemed zoned out and not too interested in much of anything. The legend goes that Ben and Jerry were friends from high school and had taken a correspondence school class in making ice cream and that is how their ice cream empire began.

I do recall that the restaurant was indeed just around the corner and was what could be generously referred to as a hole in the wall. It looked like one of those places that would get a D+ for sanitation and that was because the inspector got paid a little something from the owner so they wouldn't fail the inspections.

Something Smelled Fishy

We sat down for lunch in this seedy place and something really smelled fishy. I remember a platter of strange and odd rolled up stuff coming out and this was the oddest food I think I ever saw in front of me in my life. I felt like we were going fishing and someone served us the fish bait. But Ra El and I kept our cool about us and played along as if we were aficionados.

Sushi in the City

We nibbled on things like California roll, that at least had friendly things in it like rice and cream cheese. I remember with great clarity a powerful awareness that it was so bizarre to be sitting with ice cream icons and sucking down sushi for lunch.

The result from that day was that Ben and Jerry's sold Rachel's Brownies Ice Cream in their scoop shops for many years. We provided them with sheets of brownies that they froze and cut into irregular chunks and mixed with one of their gourmet vanilla ice creams. They tried to make it into pints but the brownies were too thick or irregular to ever get it in production. My guess is that this co-branded product existed for about five years but today it's just a chocolate blur.

What's the life lesson?

Being naive can be a blessing because you don't over analyze all the risks and rewards. You just pick up the phone and try and connect. Ben and Jerry are a couple of buddies from high school no different than Jeff and Jamie or Fanny and John or Sarah and Ellen. Don't be afraid to go for it and reach out to connect with someone who just happens to have some fame even if you think you are a *pint sized* nobody.

I guess the cliché is really true: *We all scream for sushi.*

FEARLESSNESS

I remember thinking, "What is the worst thing that could happen if I try and reach Ben Cohen? I don't get through, he ignores me and my call isn't returned." Just because someone is well-known or a public figure doesn't mean that you can't pitch them an idea. At the time, I really believed in the idea and was confident that our little humble brownie was the equal to their super premium ice cream.

This lesson in fearlessness has served me well during my marketing career. Often, I will have a new idea, product or promotion I'll want to try. I remember how easily I could pick up the phone at age 26 and call someone who was so well-known. And, I remembered the phrase; what is the worst thing that could happen to me? **Marketing requires courage**.

It requires some blindly stupid actions where you take a chance because it is hard or difficult. If you want your brand to be remarkable, do something remarkable. Be strong and take a chance.

Is there someone you feel could help your business but you have been afraid to act on it? Go for it. This is your life and you are driving. The worst case is that you can't connect with them so you really have little to lose. Maybe you have wanted to partner with another company in your field or to speak to an important thought leader in your industry.

What are you waiting for?

EASY

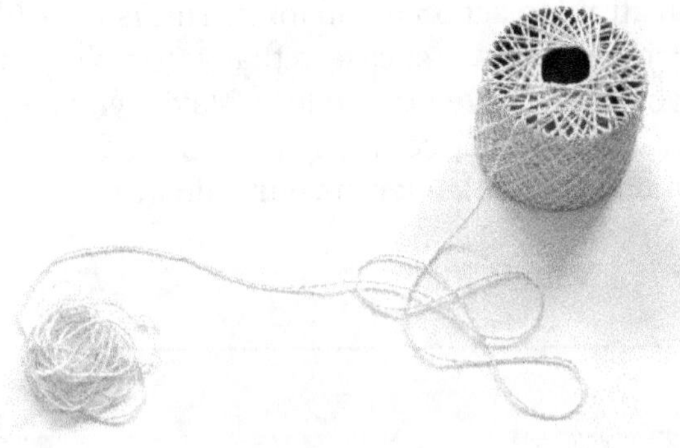

CHAPTER FIVE: EASY

ASKING THE RIGHT QUESTION

Have you ever called up your clients or customers and ask this very simple question...

What can I do to make your life easier?

I love this question and it gets at the heart of pure marketing genius where you fully understand the role you and your product or service can play in the life of your customer. Your product or service has a job (a benefit) to your customer. They may need more but haven't asked. This simple question can spark a discussion so you learn...

What else do THEY need? What else do THEY want? What new role can YOU play for them consistent with your brand and business mission?

Why don't we ask this question more often?

Do you need help?

Most companies think they understand their customers' needs. Most of us would also prefer to sell what we make but that is a recipe for a lost customer.

We often believe that things won't change. If you believe things don't change, try buying Newsweek on the newsstands or stop by the shell of an old Circuit City store. Your competitors are sniffing around trying to see what they can do to make your current customer theirs. If you don't ask this type of question, a competitor will.

What a dilemma. What an opportunity.

Confidence in Asking the Right Question

A friend of mine (who owns a small business) took my advice recently because he didn't feel close to his customers anymore. He thought my question might help him understand how he could deepen his relationship with his current customer base. I suggested that to help regain his client's confidence, he should ask his customers how he could make their lives easier. I also reminded him to be quiet after asking the question so his customer could think...then respond.

My friend shared with me that he learned so much with this one simple question. He began to truly hear what the client needed. It opened up his eyes.

He told me that from 10 calls that he made, he believes he improved his relationship with 7 of the 10 accounts. (One was out sick and the other two were on vacation).

> He learned a few things about how he delivered his service that weren't as convenient as he thought. He learned that some things he thought were valuable were actually a distraction. He learned what was on some of his client's wish lists- and it gave him some new ideas for an added service. Most importantly, he felt reconnected to his customers and gained a better understanding of how his customer viewed him and his service. Finally, his important customers got to see him as an important partner to their business.

When you ask a customer, "How can I make your life easier?", some may say they want more features for less money. They may joke about a lower price. But if you keep probing, you'll hear about undelivered value need that maybe you can serve. You may also be giving your customer more features than they really need.

Your customers are sharing pain points- something hurts and is pressuring them. True, it may be about cost but often it is about some other need within their organization. And if you aren't asking them this question, your competitor is and it may open a door for them.

So pick up the phone and call 10 customers. Ask them this simple question...

HOW CAN I MAKE YOUR LIFE EASIER?

Give them a button to push

See what transpires. You will learn a great deal, your client will be appreciative that you are thinking of them in this way and you may have a glimpse into the future.

Go ahead. It's easy.

EASY

An amazing thing happens in your marketing efforts when you ask your client how you can make their job easier. It is a simple idea and one that has served me well time after time in consulting with startups or in my corporate career.

Asking a retailer how I can design a box that would be better for his store led me to understanding my customer's need versus my need. I asked this same question to the head of advertising for Target when the company I worked for was engaged in a joint brand TV campaign that allowed my brand to gain ten times as much exposure on TV through a few minor tweaks that made things easier for them.

Easy isn't about compromise but instead it is about seeing the need from the customer/clients perspective not your own. And when my company made things easier for my customers, suddenly they wanted to work with me even more and we gain added benefits.

Asking this question is a part of an empathic form of marketing that gives you great understanding of the pressure the customer is experiencing. Sometime just by asking how you can help, shifts an antagonistic relationship into one where you are cooperating for better solutions that help both of you.

Call your client. It is really easy.

PERCEPTION

CHAPTER SIX: PERCEPTION

TEACHING MACHO MAN HO TO USE EMAIL

I have been *wrestling* with this story for a long time.

When I was a 10 years old, I remember going to a birthday party at The Newark Armory. We went to see a wrestling match featuring some of the legends of that time (1964). The star of the show was Bruno Sammartino who I thought was Superman's brother. He played the good guy and would never stoop so low that he would need a gimmick like most of the other wrestlers. You would never see him pick up a chair and slam it in the face of an opponent. He was a real athlete and had a mythic quality about him. Even his name sounded so legendary - Bruno Sammartino.

This armory was an old building back in 1964 and must have originally been used during WWII for recruitment and training. I think the place smelled liked bricks and beer. But the stage was filled with classic performers of that era like *Haystacks Calhoun, Bo Bo Brazil, Argentina Apollo* and *Andre the Giant*. These were literally larger than life athletes who provided me with hours of amusement and a strange form of entertainment. Wrestling at the time was like The Three Stooges recruited to work at the circus. It was both comical and semi-athletic with virtual no redeeming qualities. It was pure rebellious fun that in 1964 felt like anarchy. It didn't have any of the slick overproduced hype of the current productions.

The Human Circus

In this human circus the elephants and lions were replaced with huge creatures who had to work out at a gym to get their mountains of muscle. No steroid shortcuts for these guys. Oddly, something in this show connected with me since I was never the aggressive, super competitive male like these men.

I don't know what it was about this spectacle but this tragic/comic theater spoke to me. Haystacks Calhoun, who was so aptly named, was as wide as a Volkswagen Beetle and Bo Bo Brazil who was as tall as an amazon tree with limbs that could wrap around several opponents at one time. Andre the Giant, who went on to appear in one of my favorite movies (The Princess Bride), was another oversized star from that time period. Those were the days.

The mid 60's were strange times as the country was changing and culture was in a bit of shock. Keep in mind that this was the era of The Beatles on Ed Sullivan and the assassination of President Kennedy. Wrestling provided amusement, entertainment and distraction as I watched grown men apply *the sleeper hold or the flying elbow* from high above the ring. Like my fascination with magic tricks, I always wondered if the sleeper hold was real.

Thirty Years Later

Fast forward from 1964 to 1994 when I was working at GoodMark Foods in Raleigh, North Carolina. We had sold our wholesale bakery business (Rachel's Brownies) in 1989 to this Raleigh based snack food company. For the first few years I was involved with their bakery businesses. Then around 1994 I became involved in managing the marketing for their core brand of snack foods and eventually was promoted to EVP Marketing for the entire company.

Our largest brand was Slim Jim® the thin smoked meat stick that was a staple of every convenience store in America. This was a very big brand and one of the American icons in junk food like Twinkies® and Cheetos®. One of my favorite ironies from those times was that I didn't eat red meat so I was the *vegetarian* VP of Marketing for Slim Jims.

The main marketing vehicle for Slim Jim was professional wrestling and it provided the fuel to help double the brand sales and triple the company's profits.

Our Connecticut advertising agency, North Castle Partners, had brought forth an idea to use wrestling as a marketing vehicle in the late 1980's. Their logic was that a Slim Jim, like professional wrestling isn't quite real. It also represented the anti-authority image we wanted to project to young male teens (our demographic). Credit goes to Hal Rosen who was the Creative Director extraordinaire and had this inspired insight. This marketing work preceded my involvement and added credit is due to the team who worked on this before I was involved in our core business. Dick Miller, Mike Ritchie, Andy Modlin and George Stewart all played a key role in bringing this great idea to life as did many others from our marketing team. The phrase *"You guys a bit bored? Snap into a Slim Jim" became part of the lexicon during this period.* So with the strategy in place, I got the best job of all.

I got to spend time with Randy Savage AKA Macho Man.

Randy was the star of our commercials and our primary spokesperson and like my faux heroes from childhood, he was one of the superstars of the sport. Along with Hulk Hogan, Randy was truly royalty among the top wrestlers from the 70's, 80's and 90's.

Now, those who know me probably don't think I'm a professional wrestling fan.

I like to read thoughtful books, cook elaborate recipes, listens to romantic opera, drink Italian wine and watch foreign films- not your typical wrestling fan.

Truth be told, I grew out of my interest in wrestling when I was about 13 as I moved on to playing baseball in high school. I really didn't care for all the fake violence and soap opera like story lines anymore but I did know Randy Savage with his bold and over-the-top personality. He was a genuinely interesting guy and as he was an emerging wrestling star; I even knew who he was way back in the late 70's.

As a spokesperson for Slim Jim, Randy knew that he had a job to do on stage but he also had an incredibly soft heart for children who were ill and in the hospital. *I got to witness an interesting aspect of Randy.* He made it a requirement that when we would be doing publicity in a city for a Slim Jim event we would spend time visiting kids at the hospital. No one asked him why- remember he had arms the size of loins of beef- but we knew it was his way of giving a little back. He had an enormous heart but his Macho Man character didn't allow it to emerge too often. So I got to witness this conflict between the public Macho Man and the private Randy the Man. Looking back it was a real privilege to be a part of this behind the scenes experience.

One day in the early spring in 1997, I got a phone call from Randy. Now Randy's voice is so distinctive that you would never forget it. It was raspy, deep and sounded like a diesel truck backfiring. Everything always started with *Oh yeah* Brother.

My friend Britt Carter, our publicist at the time, is the only person who could mimic his voice so perfectly that he could even fool Randy. I could never tell if it was Randy or Britt on the phone.

Randy: "Jeff, I need your help with something. I want you to teach me how to use email".

Jeff: "Do you have a computer"

Randy: "Yeah, I bought one last week and I thought that you could fly down to Florida and show me how to use it. I don't want to be left behind and everyone else is using email so I figure it would be a good thing to do."

Jeff: "Cool."

Teaching Macho Man How to Email

So in 1997 I got to teach Macho Man Randy Savage how to use email. I imagined what Bruno Sammartino would think? Of course Bruno would be clueless about email but still this connected me back to my days at the Newark Armory.

Randy asked one more favor:

Randy: "One more thing - can you also teach Stephanie too?"

Stephanie was his girlfriend at the time and used the name Gorgeous George as she was his side kick in the ring. I said that I would bring my 14 year old daughter Fanny along and she could teach Stephanie and I would work with him.

So I bought some tickets for Florida and off we went down to Treasure Island where he lived. We came over to his apartment and immediately got down to work. Randy had enormously thick fingers although his hands were of average size and I worried that he would never be able to type on a key board. His knowledge of typing was pretty limited so we had to hunt and peck our way along the keyboard. We signed up for an AOL account using part of his real name which was Randy Poffo.

Fanny and Stephanie hit it off and they probably talked more about girl stuff than email. I think Fanny was all of 14 at the time but she had fun hanging out with semi-celebrities. She quickly taught Stephanie the basics while Stephanie impressed Fanny with her flashy costumes and her makeup skills.

That evening we celebrated Randy's success by going out to dinner at one of his favorite local restaurants. You would think Mickey Mantle or Michael Jordan had walked in for dinner by the reception he got. I remember him telling the maitre'd' that I was his friend who was teaching him how to use a computer and he asked him if he had an email address so he could write to him later that night for practice.

I worked with Randy over many years as our star in our commercials (Snap into a Slim Jim!) and later as our PR spokesperson for everything from the X Games with Dave Mirra, 3 on 3 Hoop It Up basketball, Country Music Concerts with George Strait and even Nascar with Bobby and Terry Labonte. Even around other super stars from music and sports, Randy was always the center of attention. Randy even got to appear in The Original Spiderman Movie and several other minor roles.

Time Goes By

Randy and I lost touch after I left ConAgra Foods in 2003. They had acquired GoodMark Foods about 5 years prior and eventually moved it to Minnesota. I stayed in Raleigh and eventually went to work at Nomaco and then at a sister company in the wine business called Nomacorc where I hang my corkscrew today.

Of the many pieces of memorabilia I kept, I had one of Randy's costumes from one of our commercials. It consisted of a cool jacket with yellow streamers, Randy's oversized sun glasses and a nifty hat. Two years ago I dressed up as Macho Man at Nomacorc for our Halloween party. I know I probably looked a little foolish but I have to admit it was an honor putting it on. The best part was the looks I got while driving on I540 to work.

This costume got around as even our Chairman of the Board, Ron Doggett, wore it at several GoodMark occasions to pump up the team. In fact, Ron wore it recently at a GoodMark reunion. We all wanted to be like Randy.

Sadly, Randy died of a sudden heart attack in 2011.

He allowed me to see that behind Macho Man was a big heart and a real human being who thought he needed to give back to kids who needed a little break from their illnesses.

Funny how eventually everything connects. Oh, yeah.

PERCEPTION

Marketing is so much more about perception than reality. The public persona of Macho Man was this ruthless wrestler who would jump from the corners of the ring and land an elbow on the throat of his competitor. The reality of this person was that he wanted to make sick kids feel better at the hospital.

A brand (or a public person) is viewed through the consumer's perception not the reality of what they stand for or who they are. You have to control that perception or image so that you can shape how current and new customers view you. Only through actively managing a brand can you control how people see you. The *facts* of what you do as a company, do not matter to the market. It is all about how you are perceived.

Do you understand all of the misperception that customers have about you and your product? Do you assume you know what they really think about their relationship with you, your customer service or product usability? Don't assume anything. Perception is how your brand is framed and you want to be able to manage and control it or else someone may drop a flying elbow on your head.

Your brand (and your business) has a reputation. Does it in fact represent what you want it to stand for? How do you know this given your biased viewpoint?

One tactical idea is to have someone ask your current customer about your brand or your business. Not as a survey or in a formal setting, but see if they can provide you with an unvarnished reflections of how they see you.. Maybe you can learn something that highlights a misperception that you need to correct.

RADAR

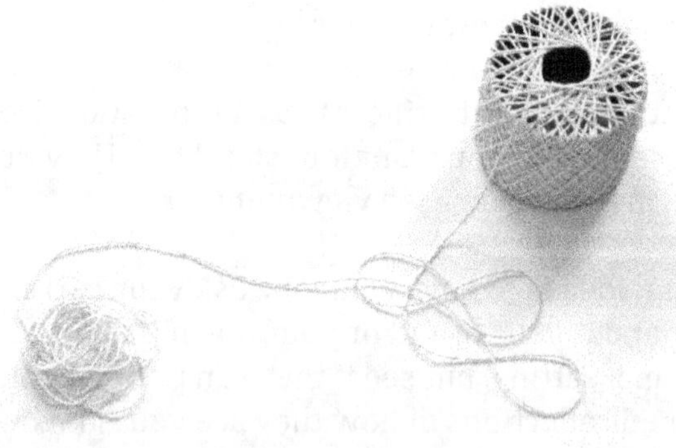

CHAPTER SEVEN: RADAR

UNDER THE RADAR

As a marketer I am often on alert to see what brand message gets through to me. How did they do that? Who told me that story that made me aware of their brand? What made me buy that product? What path was taken whereby the story of that brand broke through my own radar?

I want to learn from my experiences so I try to understand how others have reached me. I know I first heard about Tom's Shoes from my daughter Fanny but it wasn't until I heard about it from a marketing authority (Seth Godin) that I paid attention to the elegance of what they were doing. I remember reading about how powerful an influence Stumbleupon was on spreading information. But, it was a colleague who made me watch his laptop as he surfed the web in a new and different way using this cool site. I also recall tweeting about a new gelato (Talenti) that I tasted and loved and how several friends had mentioned that I "turned them on to the brand" and they tried it based on my writing. So, "Who do I influence?" and "How do I get under other people's radar?" are also of interest.

I started by examining my own media consumption behavior and brand encounters which I'll bet are somewhat similar to yours:

Television

I prefer to watch TV that is recorded. I speed through almost every commercial. It is rare that I actively watch a commercial anymore. I can't live without my DVR. My favorite buttons on my remote are mute and fast forward. On rare occasions a funny commercial or jingle will stick in my head. It takes re-watching to help remind me what brand it is associated with that commercial. How about you?

Radio & Podcasts

I love podcasts of radio shows where I can start and stop them. It is all content and no ads. If I do listen to the radio, it is for news and information. If a commercial comes on, I lower the sound or tune it out in my head. Exception to this is that I do hear the ad announcements read on NPR because they don't feel intrusive. In fact, they breakthrough since it is often the credible 'voice over' delivering the message not an advertiser.

Magazines

I don't get subscriptions to magazines at home anymore. I used to get about 10 (Time, Life, Gourmet, etc.) going back only 10 years or so. Today I occasionally read a magazine at a Dr.'s office or when I am traveling. I do look at the ads because I'm curious about graphics/copy and design. I can't believe how overpriced ad space is in these publications compared to online. By the way, if you work in marketing for a large corporation, when was the last time your CFO asked about the ROI of print advertising or attending a trade show?

I do get dozens of wine trade print magazines as I work in this industry by day. I usually glance at the table of contents and if an article is of interest, I will read it. Generally speaking I prefer reading these stories online as they are easier to pass along to colleagues. Most of the news in these magazines is old by the time I get to read it. I will glance at a few ads to see what some wine brands are doing but it feels like I am in a time-machine that is visiting a period called "old-school".

Newspaper

I no longer get a daily newspaper. I eliminated my subscription for the Raleigh, N.C. News & Observer about 2 years ago as it was of very little interest to me and it was a pain to recycle each week (I have a long driveway). The articles are also mostly free online. More importantly, there was no value to the paper version and I get more than enough news and analysis from other sources. Yes, I do miss some local stories but by not feeling obligated to read the newspaper, it has freed me so I could read more relevant blog posts or books.

Phone Calls
When I get a cold call at home or any call for that matter, I don't answer it. I let it go to voice mail unless I see a name or number I recognize. If I do pick up, I'm not very cooperative. No I do not want to take a survey about salad spinners today, thank you. I love caller ID!

Mail
I open my mail over the garbage so I can throw out the 15 credit card solicitation I get each week. (Note to Visa: you must be wasting $150 per year on me. Didn't you get the message?) Most of the mail I get that I care about comes from my mother. Any bills that can be sent via electronically come that way with a few exceptions. The inserts in the mail are just dropped in the trash. I never read them. Never!

Online
When I search online, I am more aware of the ads being promoted and the search engine optimization that was done to get high rank up in search. I think I click at a much lower rate than before. I don't remember ever clicking on a banner ad in the last 2 years. 5 years ago, I clicked very often because it was novel. Most of my online time is spent reading blogs about topics of interest to me like marketing, cooking, photography, spirituality and general business issues.

One of my social media marketing heroes, Gary Vaynerchuk likes to say that marketers screw things up for everyone. (he uses more extreme language than I do). Think of how cool email was just 10 years ago. You couldn't wait to get an email in your in box and open it. Do you feel that way today? Marketers have indeed overwhelmed us with so much coming through the digital inbox that it is easier and easier to ignore. Watch a recent presentation Gary gave in Toronto about social media and the changing landscape for media. (About one hour packed with lots of *F bombs* but worth viewing)

Customer Service

Unexpected good customer service rocks. They sneak under my radar when I'm not paying attention and when it is done well, it makes me smile and feel connected to a brand.

And of course the opposite is true too. See my recent letter to Food Lion on my blog.

Crappy experiences are like a force field that repels you from a brand. Bad service happens often. Examples abound and you could teach a college level course in B school just about "everyday bad service". Where do I begin?

Here are two recent examples.

The Bad

I waited 15 minutes in line at **Best Buy** last Sunday while 2 store employees put tape for a cash register on a shelf while I was standing in the damn line. They saw me. They acknowledged me. But putting tape on the shelf was more important than improving my in store experience. They didn't stop what they were doing and pay attention to the human being in front of them. Nope, they shelved rolls of cash register tape.

I didn't say anything as I watch the equity of their brand slowly melt away. I wanted to say two words to them: Circuit City.

When I called **Blue Cross/Blue Shield**, I was told that they couldn't call me back if we get disconnected and that I would just have to wait in the queue for another customer service person to help me. Can you imagine an outbound calling that can't make outbound calls! (Huh?)

The agent and I agreed that the best plan was for me to cross my fingers that we didn't get disconnected. (Really that was our plan)

The Good

When I went to **Whole Foods** I couldn't find two ingredients (tamarind and tahini) for something I was thinking about cooking. I approached the first person I found who worked in the store. She promptly dropped what she was doing and said she would find the manager and figure out where it was in the store and she'd come back to me in a few minutes. She did. I found what I needed and I am now telling that story to you. Talk about walking the walk.

I buy gas at a **small Exxon convenience store** in Zebulon, N.C. near where I work. When I went in last week, the young Indian woman who owns the store with her husband said to me, "We are out of the V8 tomato juice that you like but should have more in tomorrow". She remembered me. She remembered what I like to drink at lunch time even though I only fill up a few times per month. She made a connection. She must get hundreds of customers in her store each week but somehow she remembered my favorite drink. Guess where I go out of my way to buy gas and I remember that I could have had a V8?

The Ugly

I got an email recently at work from a marketing firm looking to sell me some type of social media service about personalization. The email read Dear (Fill in the Name). Seriously?

The Human Touch

The future of marketing products and services will be built on delivering a human touch to get under our radar. Dear *Fill in the blank* doesn't cut it anymore.

What steps are you taking to enchant and delight your customers with unexpected actions?

Here are two simple ideas.

Take your customer list and ask everyone in the company to write a hand-written personal thank you note to that customer for their business. Don't cross-sell or ask them to buy anything. Just say thank you and do it in a time consuming and personal way with ink and paper.

Or, find a local ice cream truck and asked them to show up at your customer's office at lunchtime to supply free ice cream. Give them a big sign that says "Thank you from (your company's name)". Don't announce it; just put the ice cream truck in their parking lot for about 90 minutes.

By the way, thank you for reading my book and passing it along to other marketers or interested small business owners.

RADAR

How can you get under the radar of your target so your marketing doesn't show? I think the big lesson is to be ***genuine, authentic and real***. Don't try and deceive someone but offer them something of value for free. Find a way to get them to talk about you because you did something special. Being *remarkable* means that people *remark* about you and. with social media, your story can be amplified.

Getting under the radar is a creative exercise. I heard a wonderful idea from an Australian marketing expert named Tim Reid who said if you are trying desperately to reach some unreachable people, consider running an ad word campaign with their name. Everyone Googles themselves. At some point, this Mr. or Ms. Fancy Pants will Google themselves and your ad can pop up on the screen costing you next to nothing. You get a chance to deliver a short message to entice them to call you. Clever and definitely under the radar.

Another idea is finding a business book that relates to a key message you want to communicate to your target audience and potential customer. I once sent 100 marketing professionals a copy of a marketing book called Different that was about brand differentiation. With the book came a sample box of our product and a hand written note explaining how our product was also different. This approach was very effective at accomplishing our two goals of putting our product in their hand and making it clear that it was different from that of our competitors.

How will you get through to your audience and stay under the radar?

LISTENING

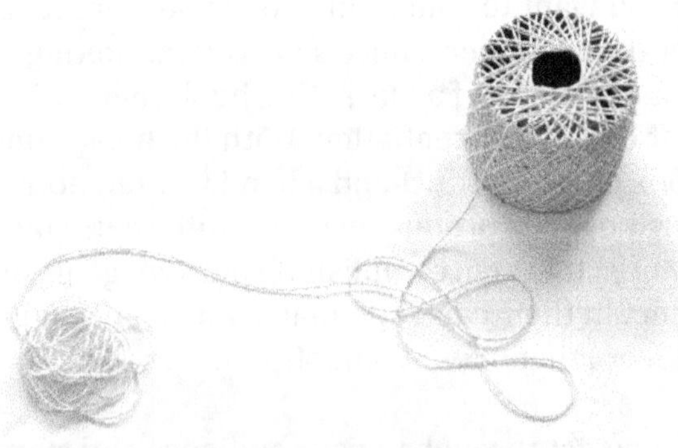

CHAPTER EIGHT: LISTENING

THE EARS, EYES AND MOUTH OF SOCIAL MEDIA

There is so much discussion about the role of social media in marketing. I'd like to offer my perspective on how to best leverage three platforms. Simply put, Facebook is the ears, Twitter is the mouth and LinkedIn is the brain.

Facebook: *THE LISTENING CORNER* I like to think of Facebook as a place for brands to primarily listen and perhaps ask a few questions. It isn't a sales environment, but it is a great place to watch and observe people who care about your category and possibly your brand. Consumers will tell you important stuff that you need to know if you shut up and listen.

Don't try and sell.

Of course it is a great place to share photos and videos but you need to be careful not to push yourself like a local TV ad. Personalize what you show; be authentic but just don't go to close the sale. You are trying to build relationships. *You wouldn't start selling to your friends at a dinner party, would you?*

If you are quiet, consumers will self-identify themselves as interested in fishing, wine or bowling. It is a great chance to observe how consumers behave and the language they use to talk about your brands. I like to think of it like a focus group you stumble upon where the subject is your product or service category. What do they say, how do they say it and what is the role a category/brand or product in their lives? *Facebook is like the ears of a brand. Shhh! Consumers behaving in their natural habitat. Be very quiet.*

Twitter: A PLACE TO ASK A QUESTION: Twitter is also a listening opportunity for brands but because of its 140 character limits, it allows you to provide short bits of information. So you get to sit in a crowded room filled with people talking about things of interest to you and occasionally you get to throw a sentence or two into the mix.

I like to use it to pose a question that stimulates discussion and/or links to a blog. So twitter is a great way to pose a thought-provoking question. How would Steve Jobs get into the wine business? What if your t-shirt could take your temperature? What if your foam insulation could sense moisture in the ceiling?

You can search key words/brands/categories means that people interested in very specific categories (hand crafted sweaters, custom designed cakes, homemade apple sauce) can find people who are talking about your products/category. If you haven't used the search function you should, it is really the great asset of Twitter. Do you know who is talking about your product? Have you ever searched for your brand name on Twitter?

Twitter is also a wonderful sharing environment for your community. Did you read a great article about some highly focused topic that would interest others? Think like a curator at a museum helping to find things of value. Don't hawk and sell stuff. Just share and provide value. For every 25 shares, maybe you can ask for something in return 1 time like a visit to your blog.

LinkedIn: THE PLACE TO CONNECT: I have been a LinkedIn user since its first year. To me, it is an incredibly powerful B2B (business to business) tool to help you understand some background about someone you want to reach. You can build highly targeted data bases of people who you want to connect with or try and meet, set up appointments or to learn a little something about their backgrounds. Its Intel central - and is rich with many ways of learning about important buyers or influencers within your value chain.

Several years ago, I used LinkedIn to help me identify 50 people who had influence over the growth of the business I worked on and they became my target list of people I wanted to follow. I used Google Alerts and other means to track their online activities. I found out when/where they were speaking to industry groups and got opportunities to meet them through this information. I saw articles they wrote and found clues to things on their mind. All of the info helped guide some of our marketing outreach programs and proved very effective in getting us to the right people.

LinkedIn is also rich in highly targeted groups interested in specific topics - commercial photographers, sticky branding or wine bloggers. Participating in those group conversations, offering insights or questions, answering requests for help and more makes it worth your time as you learn more about a targeted audience.

Ears, eyes and mouth. Social media can be a set of powerful tools if you use them wisely, learn to share and use your inside voice.

LISTENING

Great marketing starts with intense listening. You can use social media to help you hear what potential customers or clients are talking about regarding your category or brand. It isn't a sales environment but an observational space almost like a virtual focus group.

Since so much communication occurs, you can be an aggressive listener and benefit by learning about needs that exist within a segment. Sometimes it is very specific and sometimes the need isn't clear or well stated. But to improve your marketing activities you must learn to ask a question and then be quiet.

Effective sales people, those who achieve their goals, will tell you that the key to their efforts is to know when to shut up! Like music where the silences and the pauses matter, marketing requires a disciplined approach to communication with others.

Whether you are listening to conversations on Facebook, Twitter or LinkedIn, the power is asking a thought-provoking question and then being quiet. Where does the conversation go, what are people focused on and most importantly do they reveal a need as they complain?

Action: Join a LinkedIn group that focuses on your category. (Search for a key word about your market under *groups*). Join that group and then read the discussions that take place. What opportunities are being discussed where you may have a solution? Offer something of value - an example from your work or something you recently learned at a conference.

Shhh. Quiet. I'm listening.

AUTO PILOT

Chapter Nine: AUTO PILOT

TURN OFF THE AUTO PILOT

Fear.

What do you fear about your marketing efforts for the coming year? Are you stuck on auto pilot?

Fear can freeze you from acting. It can stop you from moving forward. Marketing professionals face all types of fears in their professional work. They are paralyzed as they wonder if it is worth the risk to try something new and different.

Should we launch a new product since 8 of 10 new products fail?

Is it wise to do a joint promotion with a brand with a similar audience?

Does it make sense to pull our product from our current distributor and go with a new guy in town?

Will our new virtual store interfere with our brick and mortar business and drain sales?

Should we try a new approach to meet and engage clients that have never been tried before?

Failure is doing the same thing

Every day marketing professionals stick out their necks and take a chance. It is a core part of the job. **Doing the same thing in a changing market is a recipe for failure.** Markets change. Competition steps into your world. Perceptions grow or diminish for brands. We operate in a fluid marketplace and being static is a great path toward failure.

Think of how a river flows. That is the best metaphor for your marketplace. It is constantly moving and changing. Are you in a boat navigating the flow or are you standing in the middle of the river treading water?

What can you do to help calm the fear and gain confidence in your approach?

No action, is a conscious decision

My favorite ways to manage marketing fears is to recognize that doing the same thing can be worse than trying something new and different. Products and business have a natural life cycle that may last a few weeks, months or years. But ultimately, some new force interferes with the current state. It changes the pressure, the leverage and creates a new direction.

Here is a simple exercise to help you face your marketing fears.

Auto pilot

Pretend you are sitting in a boat on a river. The engine is off. You aren't putting more fuel into the motor and you are just drifting with the flow of the water.

While on the boat, just imagine you do nothing new in your business for 12 months. No new products, no new distribution. You don't hire any new employees. You don't conduct any new promotions. No new excitement. You are forced to sit with your hands tied behind your back while your business operates on auto pilot and you get pushed along by the other boats floating past you.

After 12 months, you notice that you are no longer keeping up with the category that is growing. Boats are passing you by and you are drifting aimlessly. You notice that you have lost shelf space or facings for your products. You find a competitor gaining more press in the local papers or in the trade magazines. You notice a competitor is gaining more market awareness as you listen to more conversations in social media and no one is talking about you. Your competitor is often hiring new employees and sponsoring lots of events. Everyone else is moving forward and you are adrift.

Turning off the auto pilot

Now a year is up and you turn off the auto pilot switch and take control of the steering wheel. You immediately launch that new product that you have hesitated to sell; you hire a new PR firm to help you get your message in front of your target. You initiate a new email campaign to offer products samples directly to the clients who you have struggled to reach. In other words, you act. You take charge. You start guiding your ship (company/brand) toward your chosen destination.

I fear being on auto pilot more than I fear failure.

If I try something new to grow or expand, I expect a bumpy ride. But the downside of sitting on the sideline and not acting can only lead to me floating aimlessly. I prefer to be steering.

Face your fear. Turn off the auto pilot. Experiment with new products, promotions or tactics. Try something new and different that is harmonious with your strategy. Slowly you will find the fear disappearing as you take control of your own destiny. Marketing is fuel for your brand. **Playing it safe is the new risky.**

Go ahead. Stick a new oar in the river.

AUTO PILOT

Marketing that is on cruise control eventually will lead you to a curve in the road. If you aren't actively steering, you are in for trouble.

Don't assume that year over year the same activities will produce the same results. Markets change, competition enters and your product is moving along toward the downward slope of its life cycle.

Think of your GPS system when you make a wrong turn and the word recalculating, recalculating and recalculating. That is exactly what your marketing efforts will require.

Ask yourself this key question: If I want to keep my business growing, **what will I do differently in the coming period or year?** How can I stop doing something and start doing something else that may be more effective.

Turn off the auto pilot and take charge. Try something new and measure your results.

STORYTELLING

CHAPTER TEN: STORYTELLING

HOW CONTENT MARKETING CAN SPIKE SALES

If 2013 is about anything in the marketing world, it is about the surge of content marketing. Whether it is written, audio or video, brands have started to jump on the bandwagon to become like publishers, radio stations or TV networks. Whether you sell to consumers or other businesses, brands are waking up to the marketing magic called content marketing.

What the heck is content marketing?
Content marketing is essentially story telling. It is a critically important aspect of a fully integrated approach to marketing. Using internet business marketing tools can help accelerate leads in your funnel and ultimately spike your sales.

In simplest terms, content marketing is about creating your own story with words, video, sounds, infographics or still pictures and using them to create an engaged community of like-minded people. **At the essence content marketing is storytelling** that attracts interested prospects to learn from you.

Content marketing efforts have existed forever
The old school version of content marketing was the boring sales brochure that nobody read, cost a ton of money to produce and was filled with corporate speak and dusty unturned pages. It was *a one way communication* and suffered from chronic dullness. Sure, it was beautiful to look at but did anyone really read it? Doubtful and it really is produced to sell you something.

Even a website can be an old school format when they are static and just an online version of the corporate brochure. This type of marketing is often about promoting a category not promoting your distinctive brand promise. You may be educating people about dry cleaning in the 21st century but it's not an effective way to get the shirt off my back

Walkie Talkie Marketing

What is different about content marketing today is that it can now be a two-way conversation. I can blog about my brand and in 20 minutes I can have 10 comments from readers interested in marketing who agree, disagree or just want to share their point of view. Whether it is on Facebook, Twitter or a blog on a corporate website, the world has changed because of the ability to engage, to connect and to build more holistic relationships with customers or clients. My posts to a LinkedIn group about a topic where I have some expertise can be filled with engaging conversations and I get to share my knowledge. One of my own recent posts had 20 unique readers in less than 50 minutes.

Talking and Listening – Walkie Talkie Communications

Almost without exception, someone is interested in your niche. Whether you run an organic dry cleaners, a law firm for left handed clients or you sell lakeside property to professional bowlers, content marketing provides you the opportunity to do several important things:

STORY TELLING: Tell stories about your work and why you are different

ADVISOR: Give advice about your special knowledge or niche

SHARE: Share information that can be educational or quirky

ENRICHMENT: Enrich the personality of your brand by humanizing it

PASS AROUND: Provides an easy way for your brand to be distributed by your readers to their friends.

CONNECT A COMMUNITY: Sometimes finding like-minded individuals who share a niche interest, is the most compelling reason for content marketing activity.

HUMANIZE A BRAND: Content and storytelling allows you to be real, emotional and personal. Perhaps you can share the origin of your passion.

How can content marketing spike sales?
The problem most companies have is that they don't see how this work will translate into more business. How can there be a connection between words on a page, conversations on a podcast or video hits on YouTube. I feel your pain.

But how do you measure all of the current marketing activity you engage in? Where does your new business come from today and how do you maintain your current clients? Are you being honest with your current efforts and measuring everything you do?

Did you measure your return on that ad you ran in the local paper?

Did you measure the benefit of your new phone system and its monthly fee?

Did you calculate the ROI of that trip to an industry trade conference?

A Simple Way to Think about Content Marketing

I think that content marketing requires a simple, singular clear goal that allows you to measure progress.

An Example:

Perhaps everything you do with your marketing activities today is geared toward getting potential clients or customers to sign up for your Tip of the Week email. Today, you may have 50 people who receive your emails with 1 out of 50 calling once a month to get more information about something you mentioned.

What happens when your content marketing adds to that list and suddenly you have 250 or 500 interested people on that list? What happens when as a community, they are more engaged with your brand? What happens when instead of 1 you are getting 10 calls per month for follow up information?

This is how marketing works when you have a clear sales path defined. So all of the blogging, the podcasting, the videos or the speaking engagements all help fill your pipeline with self-identified interested leads.

Remember that content marketing and storytelling are like farming. You must plant seeds and over time, you will get to harvest the fruits of your efforts.

Marketing requires investment and patience. But ultimately you must find a way to track results. If you aren't going to create a KPI (key performance indicator) of success, than don't bother with content marketing. If you measure results with in a simple way tied to lead generation and revenue, content marketing can help grow your business.

Tell a compelling story that makes me want to learn more about you and what you do. Ultimately people buy *why* you do something not just *what* you sell. Your story is a way to emotionally connect me to your brand. So tell a simple story that helps me connect to a benefit for your customer.

Some technology companies tried to sell MP3 music players and the story they told was that they had 32 MB of audio file space.

Apple told a different story: "Put a 1,000 songs in your pocket".

So spike your sales - not your hair.

CONTENT

When you start to recognize the simple power of content marketing, it will be like discovering rocket fuel for your marketing machine. Consumers and businesses go online to search for information related to your field. They want to understand from experts and to have places for learning. **Content marketing is an opportunity for you to take your expertise and share it with potential customers and clients.**

Over time you build up information that is searchable online and brings customers to you. If you are more comfortable talking, than a podcast can be the right approach. Or, if you enjoy writing or have team members who do, a blog can be a wonderful way to share expertise. Think of content marketing like powerful magnets that draw and attract customers to you instead of old school methods like advertising that involve one way conversations. A blog or podcast gives you an opportunity to create a community online that discusses topics relevant to your industry.

Get creative and interview important industry thought leaders for your blog or podcast. The equity of their name can be leveraged as you promote these individuals. And when these well-known industry leaders are searched, your blog or podcast can show up too.

Content marketing is a worthwhile investment of time and your competitors are already doing it. No excuses. Pick up a microphone or a keyboard and get started.

QUESTIONS

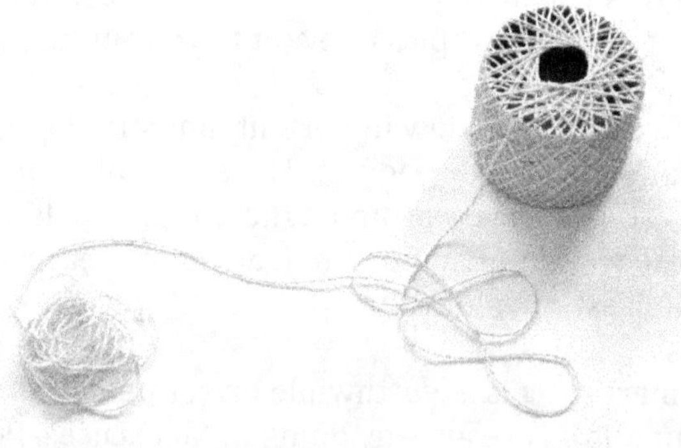

CHAPTER ELEVEN: QUESTIONS

WHY SMOKIN' JOE FRAZIER PUNCHED ME FOR 20 MINUTES

In 1974 I worked as an assistant to a commercial photographer named Larry Kanevsky in Center City Philadelphia. His studio was a second story walk up on Sansom Street. Larry was a quirky, talented commercial photographer who I met through some connections we had in common at Philadelphia Magazine. Larry was as committed to commercial photography as he was to the Viola de Gamba, a beautiful old-world cello that he played in a small ensemble. Working with Larry was my first opportunity to learn about strobe lighting, photographing inanimate objects and general commercial photography work from someone besides my grandfather. I cherished this opportunity and aspired to have a beard as cool as his.

Larry offered me a chance to help, watch and learn and in return, I offered him my unbridled enthusiasm for the craft of photography. At the time, I didn't realize I was also signing up to be a punching bag for one of the great professional boxers of all time.

One crisp October day during my third year at The University of Pennsylvania, Larry informed me that we were going to be shooting an advertisement for The Weightman Agency. Their client was a bank; GSB (Germantown Savings Bank) - The Bank that works for you. The stars of the commercial were Bill Bergey, a huge husky linebacker for the Philadelphia Eagles and boxing legend Smokin' Joe Frazier. (No 'g' on smoking- he was that cool) Bill was 6 foot 8 and Joe was 5 foot 8. The print ads we were shooting were part of a campaign that included TV and radio. I can still hear the jingle in my head...

GSB's services really knocks me out

On the morning of the shoot, I got to the studio early to help set up. The lighting was a little tricky since Larry had to evenly light two people almost a foot apart in height. Larry was a perfectionist and that is a big reason his work was so good. He would practice his studio shots over and over just as he practiced the Viola de Gamba. It had to be perfect. There often wasn't a second chance.

Larry also had a paid assistant named Phil working that chilly morning who helped him a few days per week. He stood in for Smokin' Joe and I stood on the mark on the floor representing Bill. Since I am not 6 foot 8, I stood on a step stool to simulate the height difference. The two of us posed for almost an hour as Larry worked out the lighting details. He wanted the shot evenly lit but with some light from below to make these athletes look even more imposing. At one point Larry said to the other intern Phil, "now Phil, pretend you are Joe Frazer and you are throwing a punch at Jeff. Just put your hand up to Jeff's jaw and give it a tap."

With that, in comes Smokin' Joe Frazer and a small entourage of about 11 gentlemen. In the studio was a legendary boxer who fought Muhammad Ali and dozens of elite boxers. Suddenly I hear Smokin' Joe say...

"Phil, allow me"

Joe was a pretty ferocious looking guy with arms the size of *a leg of lamb* suitable for Henry the VIII. He was small in height but he made up for it with aggression in his eyes. It scared the *bejesus* out of me.

So there I stood trying to figure out what to do and how to get this world class boxer to stop punching me. Finally, after about 20 minutes, I ask Joe to describe to me his most thrilling moment in his professional boxing life.

That stopped the *jabbing* and started the *jabbering*. He began to tell me about fighting Ali and how he knew that he was going to pull that *'rope a dope'* routine that was Ali signature move. Joe explained how his plan was to let Ali dance and dance and dance and eventually he would just land one of his awesome punches to shut him up. Watch a clip from the fight famous Ali v. Frazier fights.

At some point the tapping on my face stopped.

Joe kept on talking for about 10 more minutes but I don't remember any more of his story. My head was aching from the jabs to the jaw and I had a hard time concentrating. Getting Joe Frazier to talk was all it took to get his attention refocused on something else instead of the right side of my face.

We took dozens of Polaroid photos of me standing there with Joe and for some strange reason I can't find any of them. They may have all faded but the memory is as sharp as can be.

What did I learn?

Use the power of a great and provocative question so boxers will stop punching you in the face. **The marketing lesson is that customers will share important information about their big problem if you counterpunch them with great, provocative questions.**

QUESTIONS

Business meetings may put you in uncomfortable situations. You will want to find ways to deflect the difference in situations where someone has all the power. Great questions help to offset their energy. Be prepared, and know enough about the person you are meeting to help put them at ease or get them talking about something they know a lot about and would be willing to share with you.

When you are asking questions, people are listening to you. When you are making statements, they often won't hear you. Learn to lead with your questions and keep punching back with follow up questions. Sometimes **a simple question like WHY** is enough to get valuable insights.

Customer: *I'm not really interested in your products. They are too expensive.* **You**: *Why?*

Customer: *Your competitor was just in here last week and they are 20% cheaper than you. I have to save money this year on widgets and your high quality widgets are more than I need for my business.* **You:** *Why?*

Customer: Well we don't see people who buy at the top of the line so we can't give them as much reliability and quality as your product would provide. Now if you had a more basic model, I'd love to consider it instead since I know your firm has a great reputation.

Keep asking why until you uncover what the customer's real need is today. Your product may not be the right fit for him or you may have an alternative option that better matches his needs and your features. The right question is one of the best ways to market a product. *Don't ask me why.*

EXTRAORDINARY

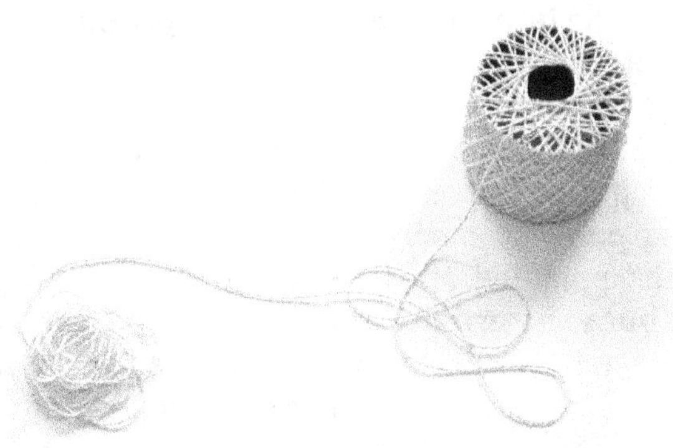

CHAPTER TWELVE: EXTRAORDINARY

THE MARKETING WISDOM OF EXTRAORDINARY FRIED CHICKEN

Jeff, please introduce yourself.

My name is Jeff and I am a chicken-aholic.

I don't mean to rustle anyone's feathers but I will admit to loving all things chicken. Sauté broiled, baked, roasted, grilled, barbecued or fried. It makes me want to cluck for joy.

This past week I got to sample some beautifully prepared fried chicken at Beasley's Honey & Chicken in Raleigh, North Carolina. I had heard (from my daughter Fanny) that it was worth the trip as she had once eaten there and spent about an hour discussing their coleslaw. This nugget of information shouldn't be a surprise - we are an odd family when it comes to food.

Staying abreast of a great product
But as in most things, the lesson was about marketing. Specifically the **importance of having a product as good as your marketing.**

So often, marketing will over-sell, over-hype and over-promote a product or service. Your expectations soar until you have a personal experience that leaves you cold, dried out and disappointed. **Marketing can only go so far to lift a product but your product must over-deliver and exceed your customer's expectations.** But how often are you disappointed when you open up a product and find that it doesn't meet basic expectations?

These are missed opportunities for the power of marketing to spread the news like gravy over a biscuit. **No one brags about an average experience on Facebook.** We do talk about products and services that disappoint us or don't live up to the hype. Spreading the word about either a bad product or its average quality does not help your cause.

I remember an ad campaign several years ago for a bank who had as part of their tag line, "we aim to make you happy." When I went to the bank and they informed me that they couldn't do something rather simple for me, I asked to have the phone number of their head of marketing since he may not have known that their aim was off.

I also remember my experience buying a Dyson vacuum. Did you know James Dyson spent eleven years perfecting the design of his vacuum. Eleven years! He wanted a product better than anyone would expect. When I first saw their advertising, I worried that the product would be disappointing. Guess what: this is one vacuum cleaner that *didn't* suck. Wow.

The biggest problem in making sure the marketing and the product are at the same level is that as owner or manager, you aren't in the best position to judge. You are too close to your business. The audience (customer) has the only vote and voice that counts. So if sales are weak or trending south, pointing blame at the marketing effort may be the wrong problem to fix. *Is your product as good as your marketing effort?*

"MARKETING IS LIKE AN AMPLIFIER.
IF THE MUSIC SUCKS, LOUDER IS NOT GOING TO HELP THINGS."

Fix your product. Make it so much better than anyone expects it to be and get word of mouth working in your favor.

Word of mouth marketing makes me think of fried chicken. Fried chicken that is dipped in buttermilk and expertly breaded and fried within a moment of perfection while it gets a lazy drizzle of honey to finish it off.

And did I mention Beasley's crisp, flaky and buttery biscuits?

EXTRAORDINARY

I don't want to tell you about an average experience I had last week. There is no reason to waste my time sharing a story about a dull department store where I bought a pair of shoes. I am sure you aren't interested in a "just okay" restaurant I visited.

But when the experience is unexpected, remarkable and surprising – I can't wait to share it with my friends, family and colleagues. Word-of-mouth needs amazement. Do you recall telling your spouse or friend about a wonderfully helpful person you talked to on the phone when you called a big company? Did they go out of their way to help you so that it shifted your view of this organization?

When you do something that truly stands out, people want to talk about it. There is social currency when I get to brag about something awesome that I found that I know my friends will also like. It reflects positively on me as curator of cool.

Invest in having the best product or service possible and let your story be told by happy tribe members who want to share the love. An extraordinary product is the best marketing on the planet especially when it precisely fits a need.

CLICHÉ

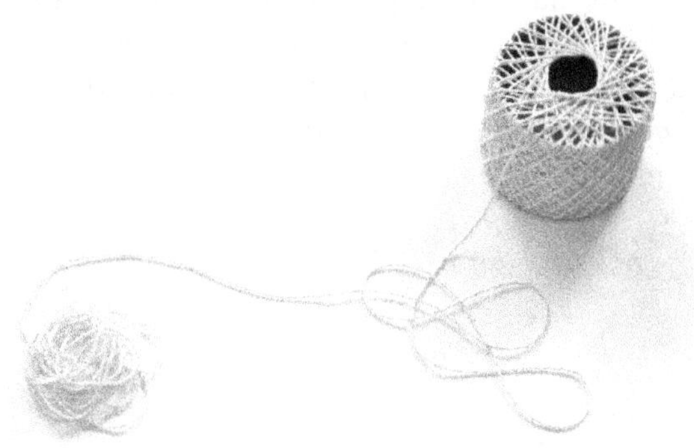

CHAPTER THIRTEEN: CLICHÉ

CLICHÉ

I work in a global marketing job and talk with my colleagues in Europe almost every day. Recently, we were discussing the printing on wine corks (that's the industry I work in) and one friend kept referring to the printing plates or marks they make as clichés. Apparently the word for printing plates or moveable type is clichés and it comes from a French origin. According to Wikipedia, it was also called a stereotype. It is also suggested that the repetitive clicking sound that a metal plate made on a press is part of the root of this word to- from the French cliquer.

Who knew?

Clichés are those things in English that are often repeated and seem trite. They have been so overused that they have lost their original meaning. But how does something become a cliché?

Are your creative messages as boring as mayonnaise?

In your content marketing*, you want to review the full list of these clichés and make sure they don't show up in your blog posts, your website, sales letters, email communication or advertising. I am listing a small sample of these but you can find the complete list online.*

Between a rock and a hard place

The customer is always right

We are here to serve you

It's all in a day's work

At the end of the day

Best thing since sliced bread.

Marketing clichés exist because we get lazy.

We decide it is easier to just stay the course, follow the beaten trail and, in any case why rock the boat? If you want to get my attention, your copy needs to ***JUMP*** *off the page and your message needs to say it in a way that I haven't heard before. Your marketing language should be filled with personality and humanity and should reflect the true values of your brand.*

My daughter Fanny is an incredible foodie. She has a blog called Fanfarefoodie. *She was struggling with a creative tagline and kept coming up with dull and boring ones that sounded like anyone could use them on a food blog. One day she came up with the phrase... "Get your Fanny in the Kitchen"*

She used something unique about her (her Fannyness- i.e. her name) and the play on words. I know I am biased but it is a great example of something unique, ownable and human. It is a descriptor from a real person named Fanny who loves to cook and it illustrates a non-clichéd approach. http://fanfarefoodie.wordpress.com/

If you are a marketer who keeps yelling at the consumer "BUY THIS!" and that you won't be undersold, then all I know about you is that what you sell and how you do business are a clichés. You are not different from the next guy and you sell a commodity.

Find language that you can own about your business. Invent words - create special content that reflects the personality of your business. Break the mold and don't blend into your category. Be original. Don't settle for the obvious. Go thirty-two miles past the extra mile to find your own voice. Hey, it ain't rocket science.

CLICHÉ

The path to being special and worth noticing can come from rich language that describes who you are in an interesting way. Fight the cliché that can make you part of a category and keeps you blending into the crowd. If everyone in your category is in a blue bag – be yellow. If everyone sells their services by the hour, offer a different approach. Don't be a cliché that is undifferentiated. **Be unique and most important; be human and a little weird.** It is okay, we are all a little weird.

Have you ever walked into a sandwich shop or deli and had a humdrum experience? Of course, we all have had typically boring Subway moments. When I went to college, we used to eat at a deli called Koch's in West Philadelphia. When we entered the packed store, Louis would walk around with sliced pastrami or turkey and give a piece to everyone waiting in line. He would remember the last time you came into the store – even if it was 2 years ago. In a "rain man" kind of way, he'd even remember what you ordered.

So many people who went to college with me tell stories about weird Louis and Koch's Deli. It was never a cliché.

BRAND

CHAPTER FOURTEEN: BRAND

WHAT IS A BRAND?

I often get to talk to different audiences about marketing and inevitably get asked about brands. What is a brand? How do you define it? What does it do for a company or a product?

The root of the word has to do with marking cattle - literally branding with a hot iron a mark on an animal to distinguish ownership. The word brand comes from an old Norse word brandr to burn. Ouch.

Simply put, a brand is a set of values.

It is an emblem that represents attributes. It isn't about the features that the products has, it represent a much higher level of benefit for the consumer or business that uses this product or service.

Brands can have shallow or deep values.

Think of a swimming pool with a deep end, a middle range and a shallow end. Some brands are in the shallow end because the values aren't well-articulated or communicated regularly.

Emotional connections strengthen brands.

The deeper the brand connection to a consumer/customer, the greater the ability to move away from commodity and category into true differentiation. Brands like Apple and Starbucks are often the best illustration of a set of values with very deep emotional bonds that keep consumers willing to pay premium prices for consistently superior products.

But what about the small to mid-sized business that wants to make its mark? How do you build a deep connection without spending millions of dollars?

I have two suggestions:

STAND FOR SOMETHING THAT CONNECTS EMOTIONALLY

You can't be just another player in a category and expect anyone to care. Find a unique and special way shows your brand doing something that reinforces your message. For example, if you are a financial services company that emphasizes that you are providing comfort to seniors in retirement, why not have as a regular activity a collection of coats and blankets for seniors in nursing homes to provide warmth to them. Your actions reinforce your message and you can share this with your clients through social media.

BE CONSISTENT IN ALL YOUR ACTIONS

You can't earn trust by showing your values sometimes and not others. **Trust is the key to great brands.** Being inconsistent won't work. Imagine a small dry cleaner that has a reputation for immaculate work and great attention to detail. What happens to your brand when your employees dress in a sloppy fashion, your signs are cheap-looking or your store front (website, Facebook page) looks disorganized or distressed? The brand's value has to be your filter or lens for everything you do.

Try this experiment.

Take two products/services in a category and try and write down how you feel about both of them. (it could be two toothpastes, laptops, automobiles, two supermarkets or two tax services). Try and find one or two words that represent the essence of your feeling and experience. Now see if there is any emotional connection and if they are inconsistent. The stronger brand will do both. You will trust the brand that connects more powerfully with you.

How well does your brand connect emotionally and consistently with your customers? Can you weave together different marketing threads to strengthen the bonds?

BRANDS

If you are going to go to the trouble of building a brand, why not take a thoughtful, deliberative approach and think about it as person. What would your brand be like if it walked into the room? Who would your brand hang out with in high school? What would your brand never do because it is against its core principles? What type of car would your brand drive? Where would you brand never be seen?

Personalize your brand so that it is well-understood by your team and ultimately your customers. Give it some depth so that you understand what it can and can't do. Can a brand like Apple also sell non-Apple PC's? Of course not. Set up rules and guideline principles of behavior that are the key values it represents. Spend time finding just the right words that will give authority to your activities and be consistent.

A brand can be the shorthand for what you stand for. Make sure you understand what those values are and don't ever move away from them or you risk diluting your brand. **Brands that sustain themselves acquire the deep and unwavering trust of their customers.**

NETWORKING

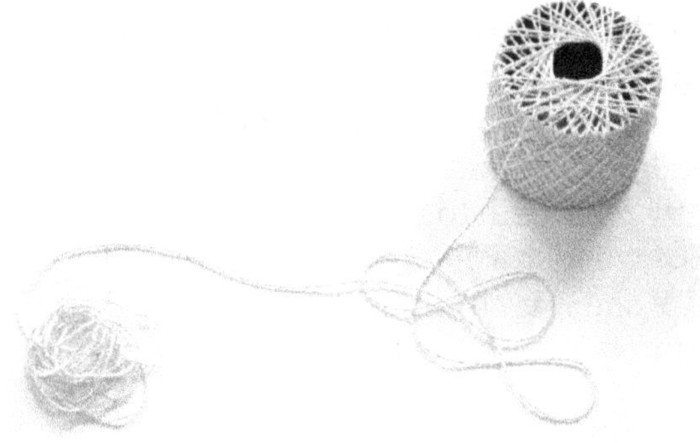

Chapter Fifteen: NETWORKING

NETWORKING SINCE AGE FIVE

When I was in nursery school at age five, my teacher foretold my future when she wrote on my report card that,

"Jeff stands out in nursery school as an especially likable little boy who is very popular with the children."

Born to Network

I loved to network and connect with marketing people even before the Internet was born. Being able to get back in touch with someone from my past that I spent a few moments, hours or days with can be valuable and very pleasurable. It takes quite a bit of work but, like many things, I have found a few techniques that have proved useful and I would like to share them. None of these ideas are radical or brilliant but they do require a modicum of discipline and focus. They also require a commitment to giving back in gratitude for the good fortunes in my own life. If you start to network actively remember to always pay it forward.

ASK QUESTIONS – The Terri Gross approach

When I meet a new acquaintance I am interested in understanding their background, their interests and most importantly their path to their current position. I ask a lot of questions. I wonder *what Terri Gross from NPR's Fresh Air would ask* if she was sitting with this person. Terri is one of the great interviewers and her questions are often more intriguing then the responses.

I am curious and I want to know more about them since it will help me understand how I might help them or someday they might help me. *How did they get to their current job?*

Why do they work at that particular company? Who do we know in common? What skills and expertise do they have or exists in their network that could be helpful to me, my company or my own network? Where did they go to school? What non-profit or extracurricular activities are they interested in. Where is their spouse working?

Information is enormously valuable yet most of us don't spend enough time in the present moment exploring our commonality during initial meetings. We are all in such a rush and I admit I get caught up in the ebb and flow too. Every encounter with someone you meet is an opportunity to ask these questions and to find out all that you can about your new contact. *Most of us just jump right into our business and ignore the human being in front of us.* Focus on the present moment, the person right in front of you and ask lots of questions.

IMMEDIATELY RECORD THE DATA

The Vitamin Approach:
Before the Internet, Outlook and LinkedIn, I used a manual system of Rolodex cards or random pieces of paper to keep in touch. Today, it is so much easier with everyone you have ever met within a few keystrokes away. My method is simple and I call it the vitamin approach. I try and record one person a day that I have met. That is five people per week or 250 people per year. I'm pretty diligent about this although I will admit that sometimes I need to catch up on the weekends. I include in the Outlook contacts free form area a few searchable terms about their personal lives, their spouse or other things I may want to be able to find in the future. This is how I have accumulated data and information on 5,341 people I have connected with over the last 20 years. Now, LinkedIn allows me to fine tune those connections and stay in touch since anyone in the system keeps their information up to date. But every day, update your contacts with the person you just met while they are fresh in your mind.

HELP SOMEONE ELSE – What can I do for you?

Finally, the third and most important tip relates to what I do with all of this information. For me, I want to be able to reconnect to help others. It is sort of like electronic mission work where someone I know might be able to help another person in my sphere. I'm not wholly selfish in doing this because I believe that if I can put positive energy out in the world, some of this help will show up for my daughters and other loved ones. Of course it feels good to help and assist but I feel a sense of obligation to pay back some of the good fortune that has come my way in life and career.

When I get random opportunities to be helpful, I ask only one thing in return and that is to pay it forward. Help someone else, link them with one of your connections and find a way to help someone else in need of assistance.

As I am writing these words while sitting at the airport in Raleigh, a young woman with a small baby comes over to me. "Jeff, it's me Jody"

Jody and I worked together almost 10 years ago. She worked at French/West/Vaughn the PR firm while I was EVP Marketing at GoodMark Foods. We live in the same part of North Raleigh and both work in marketing yet haven't bumped into each other in 10 years, although she has seen my blogs and posts through LinkedIn. She updated me on the beautiful little bundle named Lily who is snuggling against Jody. We catch up on mutual friends and connections and we share ten minutes before boarding the plane. It isn't easy to stay connected with your entire network yet Jody and I got to share a re-connection that was timely given the topic of this blog. **Networking works. Stay connected. Trust the universe.**

NETWORKING

I don't think I have any more important marketing advice than to understand the importance of networking. It enables you to find ways to help others. In helping others you will over time bring a benefit to yourself. As Jay Baer says in Youtility, marketing is about help not hype.

Can you help a friend who is searching for a job by introducing him to people in the industry he is focused on? Can it help you put a few IOU's out in the world so that someday, when you need a hand, people are willing to help you?

Networking is a way of expanding your reach, your influence and an incredibly satisfying way to do good in the world. It is a skill you have to practice each day by connecting with people you meet immediately. I try to add one new person daily, who I have connected with either in person or online to my LinkedIn network. They need to be relevant to my general field of interest but I understand the power of who they know as useful for me to help my friends and associates.

Networking in a respectful and human way, is the best marketing strategy I know to build your business.

PRICE

CHAPTER SIXTEEN: PRICE

FIVE PRODUCT PRICING IDEAS

How you price a product can help you differentiate your product or service offering. You can use a unique pricing approach as a compliment to your brand's positioning. Below are 5 ideas to consider.

Can you ask people to pay with money + something else?

What if your brand and offering provides aid and comfort to people as they age. It could be products or services. What if as part of your fee structure you offer a $100 price reduction if the customer/client agrees to donate 3 hours of time at a charity of their choice that provides services to the elderly? What a great way to live your brand instead of a plain vanilla discount. Could movie theaters offer matinee shows one day a week for the price of a 10 cans of soup? Can an accountant offer an hour of free service with every 4 hours purchased if you donate a toy for tots at the holidays? Money is but one form of currency to use.

Can you structure payment differently?

What if you sold your services like a monthly magazine subscription or an annual fee instead of an hourly rate? It could allow for better budgeting of expenses by clients and could help you avoid them feeling that they are under the clock. A marketing consultant I admire named Jim Connolly offers an annual fee for his services for small business to fit their budget. So they don't feel like they are getting pinched by the hour. Smart. Very smart.

Can they lease instead of buy?

If you have equipment you sell, would a leasing arrangement be better for the customer so that the lease brings the financing to them. Think like car sellers who take an expensive purchase and turn it into a monthly rate for a certain term. Break the price into bite size servings.

Can you give some of it away for free and charge for the bells and the whistles?

Maybe you should give away the product or service if it leads to an upgrade or it gives the user a chance to sample. Think of a food sampling in a grocery store. Would your product benefit from this approach? Many software companies follow this model. Use the product for free but then when the customer experiences the true value to them, give them the option to pay for more functionality.

Can you charge a lot more and sell a lot less?

Maybe you can sell small quantities of products or services at much higher prices and not worry about the mid-range (or low range) part of the market. Things that are very expensive have an assumed high value because "how else can they charge these prices if it isn't worth it?" Maybe you are selling your product or service short and you'd be better served selling fewer for much, much more. Price your offering for those who are willing to pay for super extraordinary service and then over-deliver value.

So grab your pricing stickers and think outside of the tag.

PRICE

How you price is powerful way to differentiate your brand and offerings. What can you do to separate yourself from your competitors? Can you borrow from others to do something different that is of value and meaningful to those consumers or businesses you want to reach.

Don't settle for what everyone else does. Find a way to delight and surprise potential customers with options that give you a leg up on your competitors.

I heard a story today on the podcast Entrepreneur OnFire about Nickhil Jakatdar. He is a software developer who was taking his product and proposal to his first client. He determined that selling it for $4,000 for a one year license was the right price. On his way to the meeting, he spoke to several colleagues and friends who all said he wasn't priced high enough. One person thought he should charge $25,000.

When he got to the perspective clients office he changed the proposal from $4,000 to $50,000.

The customer ordered two licenses. He said, "At this price, this is a real bargain".

SAMPLES

CHAPTER SEVENTEEN: SAMPLES

BITE SIZED SAMPLES

Are you ever asking the question, *"I wonder if I can do that for my business"*?

Adopting, borrowing or reconfiguring an idea from another market can be highly effective. Do you observe marketing moments as you go about your day and wonder if they apply to your marketing efforts?

While shopping at my local Whole Foods last week, I was reminded how successfully sampling works for the food industry. You give a customer a small taste of a specialty cheese and suddenly they pick up the product and put it in their shopping cart. Can you sample something in your business?

What is the equivalent of the small cube of cheese on a cracker for your business?

Is there a service or product offering that you can give to your customers in a bit sized form? A free consultation or audit is a favorite approach by many service businesses where they let you have a glimpse of what working together would be like. With physical products, getting a few samples into the hands of a potential customer can open the door to a conversation.

The power of a free sample is that it takes down a barrier to engagement with customers. It gives the service provider a chance to build a relationship with a prospective customer and it allows a connection to begin. Sometimes it is in that first step that you open several doors of opportunity.

Here are five examples where I have applied this idea of sampling to different businesses...

Accountants:
Imagine if you offer to review a prospective client's tax for the prior year for free. From your review, you will provide them with a brief summary that illustrates how you can save them money next year. Give away some of your time as a way to meet clients.

Dentists:
Imagine offering a free cleaning to a current patient who knows someone who doesn't have dental care. Have you bonded with your patient in a way that prevents them from going to another dentist, differentiated your practice and done a nice deed with little cost to you?

Electricians:
Imagine you offer a 10 point safety check free to clients who live in a very expensive neighborhood. Since they have lots of potential work, you get a chance to literally get a foot in the door and evaluate their electrical needs. Perhaps you limit the offer to the first 10 people who sign up. But what a great way to spend a Saturday going in and out of potential customer's homes, reviewing their electrical issues and most likely securing some new business.

Restaurants:
Why not offer free appetizers on Tuesday nights to teachers or fireman or emergency workers. Do it as a way to get a connected community to feel appreciated and to engage them with your restaurant. Maybe the appetizers are specially named or designed for that audience - fireman's bruschetta anyone? For a modest price you will get people spreading positive comments about your business through word of mouth.

Shoe Retailers:
How about having an hour of each day when you offer a free

pair of shoes to a homeless person for any two pair of shoes purchased by a customer. It is limited in cost but the goodwill it could generate can be wonderful for customers to post to their Facebook friends. Perhaps you have some out dated shoes that are perfectly functional - why not give someone a leg up and tie-up an emotional connection with customers?

Service Snack-sized Samples
So when you walk past the fig jam samples on toasted pita bread at your local food shop, see beyond the treat and look at how you can borrow this idea to marketing your offerings.

Sample, anyone?

SAMPLING

A powerful marketing tool that is so under used. How can you get your product or service in the hands of prospective clients - for free or at very low cost? Can you give a snack-sized serving of what you do in an effective way so a new client can take a test drive?

Free audits are ways to get closer to a potential customer. **Give something of value to let them know the benefit of working with your company.** Try to create a useful experience – virtual or in the real world. Don't wait. This is too important.

ACTIVE

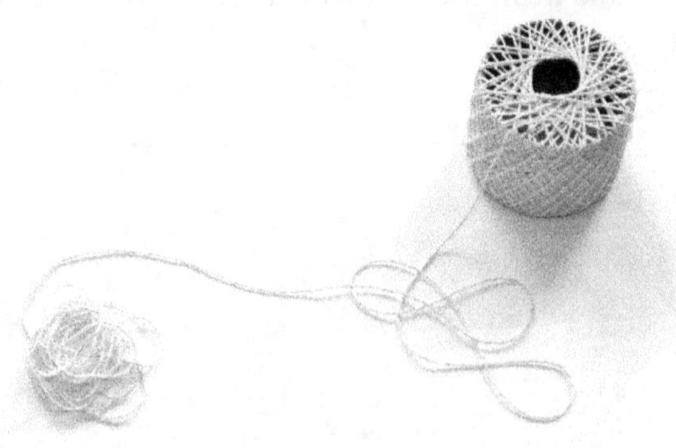

CHAPTER EIGHTEEN: ACTIVE

9 WAYS TO BE A MORE EFFECTIVE ACTIVE LISTENER

Imagine the scene. Someone organizes a meeting. An agenda is provided. You have senior leaders of the company in the room. The topic is of high importance and comes during a particularly hectic and stressful week.

Is anybody really listening to the conversation?

Check these signs to see if you are guilty of any of these indicators that you aren't present?

Is your iPhone in your hand and used during the meeting?

Do you speak before you even get a chance to think, process the comments and make certain that you are adding something necessary to the conversation?

Are you focused on your to-do-list or the next meeting instead of where you are?

Although you are physically present, are your attention and mind with you?

9 Tips:
Here are a few tips to improve your listening skills. Some are obvious and others may surprise you.

1. LAST SPEAKER: Be the last person to comment on the topic at hand. Wait until everyone else speaks.

2. 15 SECOND RULE: Wait at least 15 seconds when you are called on to speak- to gather your thoughts and make sure you know what you want to say.

3. DON'T TOUCH: Do not pick up your phone. Leave it in front of you on silent or vibrate so you can see if an emergency call comes in but don't allow yourself to touch it during the sessions. Only check your email once per hour. (I know it's hard but you'll survive)

4. BREATHE: Take deep breathes at least once every 15 minutes during the meeting to make you conscious of your breathing and mindful of being in the room.

5. PAY ATTENTION TO DETAILS: Notice a detail about each speaker so you are concentrating on them. It can be the color of a shirt or the pen they are holding. By focusing on a detail you are also putting your attention toward what they are saying.

6. SUMMARIZE WHAT YOU HEAR: Take notes that summarize strongly held points of view - not minor comments. Jim really believes we should switch distributors because of a conflict. Mary urged the team not to move too quickly on this decision without talking in person the distributor. Anne seemed ambivalent about the decision either way since she thinks the bigger problem relates to our product's price.

7. ALIGN AND REPEAT: When you do speak, an active listener will say things like, "this is what I have heard so far....Jim believes this, Mary believes that and Anne appears concerned about pricing. This restating helps you align what you heard with the speaker's intention.

8. ASK A QUESTION: When you are actively listening, you are able to understand subtle aspects of an argument. You hear in an inflection some willingness to compromise, to shift positions or to consider more information. Active listeners succeed because they see new paths forwards. Consider a question instead of a statement when it is your turn to talk.

9. DON'T GO TO THE MEETING

If you are struggling with paying attention during a meeting, perhaps you shouldn't attend. Sometimes it is important to get clarity about where you need to spend your time. Perhaps your distraction is well-placed and your attention needs to be on another more important issue. Just say no.

This Moment
Listening is about being present in the moment. Your past is gone. The future hasn't arrived. All you have is the moment. By listening and being self-conscious of what is going on right now you and your colleagues will benefit with better actions.

Can you hear me now?

ACTIVE

Are you fully present and paying attention during meetings with colleagues or customers or suppliers? If you are on your iPhone or reading emails, you can't possibly be getting the most out of your time. Being an *active* listener is a key to becoming a successful marketer because it means that you are developing the skill to understand your key target audience and to really hear what is important to them.

Practice listening without offering opinions. Quietly absorb information without feeling like you need to share your point of view. Consider the work like an anthropologist who is studying another culture. Watch. Observe. Record. But don't let the idle chatter in your brain interfere with the need to pay attention. Focus.

Listening is a powerful tool for those who are interested in a marketing career. In fact, if you are truly listening you will hear the opportunities emerge. Being an active listener means that you are truly hearing what your customer needs not what you are trying to sell them. It gives you an advantage and most inexperienced marketing professionals don't appreciate its power. **My advice is to stop talking so much and give yourself an advantage.**

We can stop seeing by closing our eyelids. But we can't turn off our ears since we don't have ear lids. There is an evolutionary reason for always being able to hear. *Shhh. Please be quiet.*

PROMISES

Chapter Nineteen: PROMISES

Marketing Promises

It is a funny thing how marketing is something every business needs but you don't really want it to be seen. Marketing is like the fuel in your car. It gives you the energy needed to move forward but who wants to focus on the gasoline?

Local car dealers allow their marketing to show so much that most of us react by hitting the mute button. Marketing shouldn't be in the forefront and it certainly shouldn't be annoying. *So what is the essence of this thing called marketing?*

The essence of any marketing activity is the idea of fulfilling a promise.

Promises through Stories
Businesses big and small need to tell stories that connect with customers. They need to be effective at delivering key messages, benefit information and influencing buying decisions. But marketing isn't something you want showing because it is a part of a delivery system.

Think of a train.

Is your experience of taking a ride on a train about the seats or the speed you travel? Is it about getting WIFI connection or being able to read in silence? Well, yes, yes and yes. What the train ride isn't about is the mechanics of it all. You don't really care about the engine, the diesel or how it works to transport you from point A to B.

Marketing should be about the *ride* not the engine

The people you are trying to reach are not thinking about you. They have needs, problems and issues. They are open to someone telling them a story that fits precisely with their need. They have locks that need keys - use whatever metaphor you like but it is the marketer's responsibility to explain what unspoken need you can fix. They may learn about you on a blog post, from a friend or through a professional acquaintance.

Your marketing isn't showing if you are doing what Wayne Gretzky used to describe about playing hockey---

Skate where the puck is going.

BRANDS SHOULD MAKE A PROMISE AND KEEP IT

Here are three needs and promises to illustrate this important marketing concept.

I NEED MY OIL CHANGED. I want it done quickly. I don't want to be pushed into buying a lot of other stuff. I want an expert who can handle the problem quickly. **Jiffy Lube** solves this problem and was first to do so. Their promise is quick oil changes and for more than 15 years they have kept that promise to me.

I DON'T FEEL WELL AFTER MY DOCTOR'S OFFICE HAS CLOSED. It is the weekend. It isn't easy to get to see my doctor. What do I do? **Urgent Care** solves this problem. It meets a unique and special need in the health care market. It isn't a hospital, a specialist or an emergency room. Yet, it does a little of all those things. It is medicine delivered during off-hours.

MY BUSINESS NEEDS A LOW COST WAY TO PRODUCE FANTASTIC VIDEOS:

Your marketing budget is drained and you need to create a fantastic video about your cooking classes that you do in a consumer's home. You can't afford to hire a professional but you need something to use on social media to get the word out.

Animoto is an easy to use online software video service allowing you to tell a story with your pictures, videos and music that feels like it cost $10,000 when it only cost $20/month. Here is an example of an Animoto video in case you are unfamiliar with what they offer. An example of Animoto video from Fanfare, a Wilmington, North Carolina Caterer

What problems are you promising to fix for your customers?

PROMISES

Your brand, product or service has to stand for something bigger than itself. The promise is the ultimate benefit that you fulfill for your customer. Think of fulfilling a promise like a pain killer versus a vitamin. It goes right to the customer's need, to where it really hurts and where a solution doesn't exist. It isn't slow acting and gradual like a vitamin might be over time.

A promise isn't marketing mumbo jumbo. It is what the brand represents and stands for in your distinctive way. Your work fulfills the promise you make with every sale you make to a customer. Fulfilling a promise isn't trivial but core to being successful at marketing.

I promise this is true.

BLANK

CHAPTER TWENTY: BLANK

STARTING FROM SCRATCH

A blank piece of paper
When you are putting together marketing plans for a new product or your annual brand plan, do you build on what you did last time or start fresh? Are you a fan of the blank slate? I believe that starting with a clean piece of paper is so important because it forces you to recommit to each decision.

Is advertising still relevant to your target?

Should promotions be increased versus an email campaign?

Are you willing to keep investing in that trade show that keeps disappointing you with weak results?

Can you do more with events that will build your brand awareness among key thought leaders who can help spread the word?

Are your marketing actions working based on your success measurements?

The counter-argument to starting with a blank piece of paper is, "why reinvent the wheel"? Why go to the trouble of starting over and rethinking each decision?

I can think of 5 reasons to reinvent the wheel.

GET NOTICED: How will you be noticed if you continue to do the same thing over and over again?

STAND OUT: If everyone is using "the wheel", how will you stand out from your competitors and not blend into the category you belong to?

DELIGHTING YOUR CUSTOMER: When customers expect you to do something one way, you have a chance to delight and surprise them if you change gears.

WHERE ARE YOU GOING? Maybe the things you did last time didn't take you where you wanted to go? Why keep doing it?

SAY SOMETHING FRESH: Your brand or products are trying to make a statement, why not say something fresh and new with a disruptive approach. Breakthroughs require a jolt of the unexpected. **We pay attention when expected patterns are disturb.**

So if you are launching a new product or service or developing plans for the coming fiscal year, maybe you should start without tying yourself to the past unless you can justify that it will help you get to your future.

Pedal on, pedal on.

BLANK

Things change. And then they change some more. You have to readjust your plans to the current situation. If you are doing what you did previously, you may be not be adapting to the current environment.

A new competitor enters your path. You suddenly have someone undercutting your price or offering free delivery when you charge. If you are doing the same thing as before with the declining results, you have to reassess with a blank piece of paper what your marketing plans should be.

Don't be afraid of the blank page. It is a fresh start to get to the next level.

EXUBERANCE

CHAPTER TWENTY ONE: EXUBERANCE

WHAT FRANK ZAPPA TAUGHT ME ABOUT MARKETING

In my teenage years, I started to shift my heroes from sports figures like Tom Seaver, Joe Namath and Sandy Koufax, to the musical genius Frank Zappa. I think it was my first true awareness of marketing as I knew he was doing something differently. I could always depend on Zappa to follow the unbeaten path. He helped me to understand how and why *different* mattered so much. I never saw him as a publicity seeker- rather he was just following his inner Zappa.

When I was in college at The University of Pennsylvania, I got to photograph Zappa live on stage at Irvine Auditorium around 1977, as he regaled the audience with irreverence and laughter. It was a thrilling experience to be behind the scenes watching him perform. If you could have bottled the energy, you could have lit up a city!

But like a thread running through the tapestry of my own education, Zappa taught me some important things about branding and weaving my own material.

Strictly Commercial

As a kid, Zappa's father worked for the military industrial complex involved in gaseous chemical. Themes around germs, warfare and the like were ever present in his music. His father worked with mustard gas and I have read that they kept gas masks in his home. Some of Zappa's childhood illnesses appear to be related to living so close to the manufacturing factory. I am certain this has something to do with how he viewed the world and lived each day. He wasn't just against the norm but he delighted in the way a creative spirit could shine a light and provide direction for a life's journey.

Avant-Garde

I learned the word avant-garde through listening to Zappa as names like Edgar Varese, Igor Stravinsky and the doo wop bands all shaped his musical vision. Growing up in LA, and with his own diverse background, Zappa rejected all things mainstream in music and politics as he would quote from the Mad Men era Jell-O jingles or other commercials of the day. He made fun of everything and everything to him was fun.

Watching him perform was like seeing inside the mind of a joyful child who never left the playground.

His music was like nothing I had known. How he lived in the world was so idiosyncratic and odd that it amused me beyond words. His music was always difficult to categorize which was a clue to his marketing genius. He didn't want to be seen in anyone else's mold or style. He was, in his personal and professional life, an expression and realization of something completely different.

As a self-taught composer, musician and persona, it was always nearly impossible to describe him. His first album, Freak Out! with The Mothers of Invention was rock and roll, improvisation, jazz-like and a collection of sounds that interested him from the audio panels. To call him an iconoclast is an injustice to his spirit as labels never fit. He was just Zappa.

So how does all this fit with marketing?

If I could sum it up, the following 5 themes were baked into my childhood and formed a key part of my own approach marketing. Thanks for the jump-start Frank and for setting off a lifetime of creative sparks.

Be Real
Let whatever is inside of you out and be proud of the way that you can uniquely create something of beauty, of value and that delights a small tribe.

Be Fresh
Don't be the same as everyone else clamoring for attention. If the world is zigging, don't just zag but fly somewhere above the rest. Wiggle when everyone marches straight forward. Make sounds with your hands when it is time to be serious.

Be Inventive
Let go of judgment. The question isn't whether it is good or will anyone like it or will it be a success. The question is are you being truthful to your own world view. Enjoy the sheer pleasure of the creation process and realize that your time on earth is so short that fear is just a bug on a windshield as you fly down life's highway. I'll bet Steve Jobs had Zappa as a soundtrack in his life.

Be Bold
Experiment, blend, synthesize, try and fail and try and fail and fail and fail and fail until you cry. But don't just fall into lock step with everyone else. Be proud of saying that you tried something novel.

Be Exuberant
Celebrate the joy of light, sound, movement, words and humor. Of all the lessons about marketing that I channeled from Zappa, the key was to celebrate and delight in the sheer joy of ideas and daily life. Find a voice that allows you to express the brilliance of your own life.

Zappa was an ever present hero of mine as I grew up in suburban New Jersey and during my days in Philadelphia during college and beyond. It was as if he gave me and my friends Jamie and Larry permission to express our creative self through many forms. But it was always in the anti-establishment and irreverent way of being that helped spark my own creativity in both business and life. Be frank...sort of a worldview urging me to find my own unique voice and approach.

And to this day, I still watch out where the huskies go and don't you eat the yellow snow.

EXUBERANCE

Whatever you are marketing, do it with an *exuberance* that lets customer feel your great joy, sparkle and aliveness. Don't you want to be around people who exude a passion for what they are doing whether they are fixing your air conditioning, putting hair conditioner on your scalp or selling you insurance?

Passion is the best engine for marketing anything. If you aren't connecting to your own passions in your work - do something else. Find that path to be filled with an enthusiasm for what you are doing and business will come your way. I lived this and found it to be absolutely true.

Who wants to buy from someone dull and bored? Listen to Zappa and fill your work with your heart.

LESSONS LEARNED

LESSONS LEARNED

This book explains the fundamentals of marketing through my personal life stories. I illustrated the vital role that **focus** plays in helping to narrow the field of possible products and services you offer. Focus can be very liberating as it narrowly defines your offering and concentrates your efforts.

Optimism in your approach and attitude toward your effort also enables you to meet the challenges and failures that will come your way. Optimism is a superpower giving wings to your persistence.

Fearlessness is another attribute of marketing that gives you permission to try things – as crazy as they may be, without fear of failure. I would rather work with fearless people whose courage inspires me and whose passion ignites their ability to keep trying.

When you ask the right questions, you can help make life **easy** for customers. It is a powerful thing to help someone solve their pain in a way that requires little from the customer except money. Making things easy for others is valuable and you should be paid commensurate with the ease your deliver.

If marketing is anything, it is about the **perceptions** that occurs *not* the reality. Your product or services is positioned in your targets mind and that perception is all that matters. Your efforts are defined and restricted by perceptions and you want to get out ahead of that to define your brand first before a competitor does that for you.

When you get under someone's **radar** it means that your message is reaching your audience. When you are being helpful in providing utility and value, your audience is open to listening and hearing what you have to say. Getting under the radar isn't being deceptive but it is about delivering a message of value at the right time once trust and credibility are established.

Social media are primarily **listening** tools providing you with great opportunities to hear and understand gaps and needs in a market place. They aren't soapboxes to stand on and sell. Think of them as listening booths of opportunity.

Targets are narrow and very specific groups. Woman ages 29-54 are not a target. A target is a single mom named Shirley, age 35 who own dogs, has three kids, shop at Target not Wal-Mart, like to cook and entertain and vacation frequently at National Parks. Targeting helps when you have specific individuals in mind that helps you understand their emotional needs, personal habits and purchasing motivation.

When your marketing is on **auto pilot**, you are ignoring the changes in the marketplace. Like a GPS, you have to keep recalculating, recalculating and recalculating to help you get to your destination as roadblocks obstruct your path.

Content marketing is magnetic. It brings interested customers towards you to learn about you, your business and your offering. When you blog about inventive light, local and savory dishes, customers interested in that style of catering will find you. Whether in words, photos, videos or podcasts, content in the right context is the most powerful fuel for your marketing vehicle.

Being **provocative** in your questions to customers helps you get deeper into a customer's real needs. Do they really have a need for your product or service or is something more emotional going on that leads them to want to buy that handmade purse, custom motorcycle or weekend getaway. Ask interesting questions that probe to truly understand motivation.

Be **extraordinary** at something. My wife and I were at making sinfully-rich double brownies. Others are special at providing counseling, teaching yoga or offering legal advice.

Don't blend into the category and be like everyone else. Find something that allows you to separate from your category. Brands become important when they put distance between themselves and commodities. Being extraordinary is critical toward that differentiation.

Clichés dull the senses. Words have explosive power when used wisely to describe what you do. Find ways of explaining your business that are memorable and not the language of the ordinary and every day. Create sparks when people learn about you to ignite interest.

Brands matter. They are the shortcuts that are emblems representing value, trust and credibility. Don't treat your brand as an afterthought but as the most valuable asset of your business. It as a symbol representing why customers should buy from you and shorthand that represents the value you provide.

Networking is a marketing trampoline that can catapult you to new levels. Never miss an opportunity to ask someone how you can be helpful to them and to expand your reach of giving. That network will prove invaluable and you want to dig that well now before you get thirsty.

Don't **price** below the value you provide to others simply to make a sale. Price telegraphs value and worth. If you are too cheap, customers will expect poor quality. If you are in fact offering something better and different from your competitors, if it is valued then you will be paid for it. Don't build into your price more than your customer value. No one benefits.

Everyone likes a snack. Can you **sample** your product, your service or your ideas so you give away a bite-sized trial? Software companies offer free versions of their work to give you a taste of what it is like to use their product. Grocery stores sample foods to get you to try their tasty delights.

What can you sample to get customers to learn firsthand of the benefit you offer?

Marketers, who learn to listen effectively, succeed. They hear opportunities. They observe needs. They see gaps in the marketplace. Stop talking. Ask a question and listen really carefully to how a prospect responds. That is marketing at its finest and requires **active listening** skills.

A marketing **promise** is the simple commitment you make to a customer. When people have needs, a brand can fulfill it with a promise. You have a pain and I have pain pills that can fix that pain. Promises go right to the root of a need and offer something to help heal and fix what ails.

Marketing plans require fresh thinking. If you start from a **blank** slate, a clean piece of paper or an open word document, you can reimagine everything. Allow yourself the joy and power of refreshing your approach. The market will reward you.

The **exuberant** marketer is vividly alive and experiences great pleasure from the work and value they provide. They offer excitement, explosions and energy that inspire others. Expressing the full potential of what you have to offer in your own personal way is how great marketing is realized. Don't hold back. Be your true self and let the unbridled joy show each and every day.

CONTACT ME:

If you are interested in learning more about me and my work, please visit my blog called MomentSlater at **http://momentslater.blogspot.com/** or at LinkedIn at **www.linkedin.com/in/jeffreylslater/**

You can follow me on Twitter at **@Moments_Later** or on Instagram **@moments_later**

You can email me at **jeffreylynnslater@gmail.com**

If you are interested in council, advice or coaching, you can set up time to speak to me through **https://clarity.fm/jeffreyslater**. My fees for service are donated to Charity Water.

Would you **write a review on Amazon**? Your feedback is enormously helpful and is the best gift an author can receive.

Thank you for reading Unraveling the Mysteries of Marketing.

How can I help you?

Listening
Cliche
Extraordinary Easy
Storytelling Samples
Optimism Fearlessness
Focus Questions
Autopilot
Active Targeting
Blank Perception
Networking
Price
Promises
Exuberance Brand
Radar

www.ingramcontent.com/pod-product-compliance
Lightning Source LLC
Chambersburg PA
CBHW051315170526
45166CB00002B/559

* 9 7 8 1 4 9 2 8 4 5 9 0 4 *